Anonymous

The Echoes of the Lakes and Mountains, or, Wonderful Things in the Lake District

Being a companion to the guides

Anonymous

The Echoes of the Lakes and Mountains, or, Wonderful Things in the Lake District
Being a companion to the guides

ISBN/EAN: 9783337317669

Printed in Europe, USA, Canada, Australia, Japan

Cover: Foto ©Lupo / pixelio.de

More available books at **www.hansebooks.com**

THE ECHOES

OF THE

LAKES AND MOUNTAINS:

OR

WONDERFUL THINGS

IN THE

LAKE DISTRICT.

(Being a Companion to the Guides).

EMBRACING :—

ANTIQUITIES — ROMANTIC LEGENDS — PHENOMENAL MARVELS — GRAVES AND EPITAPHS—OPTICAL ILLUSIONS AND MARVELLOUS ECHOES—PICTURESQUE SPOTS AND PLACES—ECCENTRIC CHARACTERS NEW AND OLD RECORDS AND ANECDOTES OF THE ILLUSTRIOUS MEN AND WOMEN WHO HAVE MADE IT THEIR HOME,

WITH PORTRAIT OF "MARY OF BUTTERMERE," AND VIEW OF THE "FISH" INN, BUTTERMERE,

BY AN
"ANTIQUARIAN, GUIDE, PHILOSOPHER AND FRIEND."

" WHEN FOUND MAKE A NOTE ON'T."

LONDON:
JAMES IVISON, 22, WARWICK LANE, E.C.

PREFACE.

ALL the Counties of England are rich in interesting and romantic incidents, but none so rich, rare, and varied as those of Cumberland and Westmorland. The "Wonderful Things" unfolded in this little volume will amply bear out the assertion. The only merit we claim is for the labour of our research, and the bringing to light marvels that have existed but have been hidden by the lapse of time. As Kingsley says on the value of Books:—"There is nothing more wonderful than a book!—a message to us from the dead—from human souls whom we never saw, yet who lived; and yet these, in the little sheets of paper, speak to us, amuse us, terrify us, teach us, and comfort us." We hope this description of a book may be applied to the one we now commend to the readers' attention. Time has consecrated and age made gray the numerous collection of the rare gleanings of our volume, and if the interest inspire the reader as much as the gleaner of them, he will not be content with the perusal of our collection, but enlarge his acquaintance by a visit to the spots, places, and antiquities, that have so much fascinated us.

INDEX.

	PAGE
Abbots of Furness	65
Ancient uses of Blacklead or Wad	101
An old Piano's Apology	149
Ben Wells, the Wonderful Dancing Master	84
Borrowdale Cuckoo, The	65
Borrowdale Eagle Stories	91
Bowder Stone, Borrowdale, The	61
Buttermere and Penny Postage	31
Cataract of Lodore, The	46
Celebration of Rushbearing at Grasmere Church, The	114
Christmas in Cumberland	78
Crosthwaite Church and Southey's Tomb	142
Cumberland Lasses at the Royal Agricultural Society's Show, at Carlisle, in 1880	31
Cumberland Moss Troopers	81
Cushion Dance, The	89
Danger of Ascending Mountains in Winter	44

	PAGE
De Quincey	137
Derwentwater	37
Dr. Brown's Picturesque Description of Keswick... ...	106
Druid's Circle, Keswick	62
Dunmail Raise	49
Echoes of the Lakes and Mountains	76
Engraver of the Rocks, The...	133
Eskdale	148
Fox How, the Lake Residence of Dr. Arnold	138
Giant of Troutbeck Park, The	85
Giant's Grave, The	100
Graphic description of a Stag Hunt in 1773	128
Grasmere	151
Great Bull Fight, A	89
Hartley Coleridge	154
Helm Crag, Grasmere	150
Helvellyn	42
Hogarth's Father's House	87
"John Peel," The Popular Hunting Song...	145
Keswick or Derwentwater Regatta in the Olden Times ...	54
Kirkstone Pass	147
Lament of the Border Widow, The	115
Leven's Hall	152
Life of John Hatfield, and his Marriage with Mary of Buttermere, The	1
Little Langdale	153

	PAGE
Martineau's, Miss, Description of Professor Wilson	98
Mirage on Skiddaw, A	50
Modern use of the word " Lake "	104
" Mortal Man " Inn, The	86
Mountain Deluge, A	74
Mrs. Heman's Home on Windermere	90
Old Cumberland Proverbs	83
" Old Man," Coniston, The	148
Only Cumberland Martyr, The	80
Only One	155
Optical Illusions	127
Poet Gray's Beautiful Description of Grasmere, The	96
Poet Shelley's Residence at the Lakes, The	121
Pope's Lines on Windsor Forest	156
Professor Wilson at Wastdale	136
" Punch " and the Poet Laureate—Wordsworth	131
Regatta on Derwentwater, 1782	124
Remains of Painted Glass in Bowness Church	126
Ride over Skiddaw in 1794, A	68
Rocks of Lodore, The	135
Roman Remains	124
Romantic Tradition of Egremont Castle, A	117
Rushbearing	157
Rydal	147
Samuel Taylor Coleridge's Opinion of Scotch and English Lakes	156

Siege of Carlisle by "Bonnie Prince Charlie," The	118
Sir Walter Scott's Memorable Visit to the Lakes	103
Skiddaw, Keswick	35
Souther Fell—Its Phantom Army Mirage	39
Southey and Autobiography	154
St. Herbert and his Isle	56
Storr's Hall, Windermere	152
Thomas Carlyle	148
Threlkeld Tarn	34
Threlkeld Hall, and the Castle Rock, Vale of St. John	33
Tourist and his Dog, The	108
Troutbeck, Windermere	152
Two Ancient Cumberland Ballads	97
Unfortunate Earl of Carlisle, An	82
What is a Mountain?	64
Wishing Gate, Grasmere	151
Wonders of Saddleback, The	59
Wordsworth at home	88
Woto Bank	144
Wythburn	157
Yew Trees	36

THE LIFE

OF

JOHN HATFIELD,

COMMONLY CALLED

THE KESWICK IMPOSTOR;

AND HIS MARRIAGE WITH

MARY OF BUTTERMERE.

THE subject of the following pages (who acquired the appellation of the Keswick Impostor,) whose extraordinary villainy excited universal hatred, was born in the year 1759, at Mottram, in Longdendale, Cheshire, of low parentage, but possessing great natural abilities. His face was handsome, the shape of which, in his youth, was oval, his person genteel, his eyes blue, and his complexion fair.

After some domestic depredations (for in his early days, he betrayed an iniquitous disposition), he quitted his family, and was employed in the capacity of a rider to a linen draper, in the north of England.

In the course of this service, he became acquainted with a young woman, who was nursed and resided at a farmer's house in the neighbourhood of his employer. She had been, in her earlier life, taught to consider the people with whom she lived as her parents. Remote from the gaieties and follies of what is so idly denominated polished life, she was unacquainted with the allurements of fashion, and considered her domestic duties as the only object of her consideration. When this deserving girl had arrived at a certain age, the honest farmer explained to her the secret of her birth; he told her, that notwithstanding she had always considered him as her parent, he was in fact only her poor guardian, and that she was the natural daughter of Lord Robert Manners, who intended to give her one thousand pounds, provided she married with his approbation.

This discovery soon reached the ears of Hatfield. He immediately paid his respects at the farmer's, and having represented himself as a young man of considerable expectations in the wholesale linen business, his visits were not discountenanced. The farmer, however, thought it incumbent on him to acquaint his lordship with a proposal made to him by Hatfield, that he would marry the young woman if her relations were satisfied with their union, but on no other terms. This had so much the appearance of an honourable and prudent intention, that his lordship, on being made acquainted with the circumstances, desired to see the lover. He accordingly paid his respects to the noble and unsuspecting parent, who conceiving the young man to be what he represented himself, gave his consent at the first interview; and, the day after the marriage took place, presented the bridegroom with a draft on his banker for £1,500. This transaction took place about 1771 or 1772.

Shortly after the receipt of his lordship's bounty, Hatfield set off for London; hired a small phæton; was perpetually at a coffee-house in Covent-garden; described himself to whatever company he chanced to meet as a near relation of the Rutland family;

vaunted of his parks and hounds; but as great liars have seldom good memories he so varied in his descriptive figures, that he acquired the soubriquet of *Lying Hatfield.*

The marriage portion now exhausted, he retreated from London and was scarcely heard of until about the year 1782, when he again visited the metropolis, having left his wife with three daughters she had born to him, to depend on the precarious charity of her relations. Happily she did not long survive: and the author of her calamities, during his stay in London, soon experienced calamity himself, having been arrested, and committed to King's Bench prison for a debt amounting to the sum of £160. Several unfortunate gentlemen, then confined in the same place, had been of his parties when he flourished in Covent-garden, and perceiving him in great poverty, frequently invited him to dinner; yet such was the unaccountable disposition of this man, that notwithstanding he knew there were people present who were thoroughly acquainted with his character, still he would continue to describe his Yorkshire park, his estate in Rutlandshire, settled upon his wife, and generally wind up the whole with observing how vexatious it was to be confined at the suit of a paltry tradesman for so insignificant a sum, at the very moment when he had thirty men employed in cutting a piece of water near the family mansion in Yorkshire.

At the time Hatfield became a prisoner in the King's Bench, the late unfortunate Valentine Morris, formerly governor of the Island of St. Vincent, was confined in the same place. This gentleman was frequently visited by a clergyman of the most benevolent and humane disposition. Hatfield soon directed his attention to this good man, and one day earnestly invited him to his chamber; after some preliminary apologies, he implored the worthy pastor never to disclose what he was going to communicate.

The divine assured him the whole should remain in his bosom "Then" said Hatfield, "you see before you a man nearly allied to the house of Rutland, and possessed with estates (here followed the old story of the Yorkshire Park, the Rutlandshire property, &c., &c. ;) yet notwithstanding all this wealth (continued he), I am detained in this wretched place for the insignificant sum of one hundred and sixty pounds. But the truth is, Sir, I would not have my situation known to any man in the world but my worthy relative, his Grace of Rutland. Indeed I would rather remain a captive for ever. But, Sir, if you would have the goodness to pay your respects to this worthy nobleman, and frankly describe how matters are, he will at once send me the money by you, and this mighty business will not only be instantly settled, but I shall have the satisfaction of introducing you to a connection which may be attended with happy consequences."

The honest clergyman readily undertook the commission; paid his respects to the Duke, and pathetically described the unfortunate situation of his amiable relative. His Grace of Rutland, not recollecting at the moment the name of Hatfield, expressed his astonishment at the application. This reduced the worthy divine to a very awkward situation, and he faltered in his speech, when he began making an apology; which the Duke perceiving, he very kindly observed, that he believed the whole was some idle tale of an impostor, for that he never knew any person of the name mentioned, although he had some faint recollection of hearing Lord Robert, his relation, say that he had married a natural daughter of his to a tradesman in the north of England, and whose name he believed was Hatfield.

The reverend missionary was so confounded that he immediately retired and proceeded to the prison, where he gave the impostor, in presence of Mr. Morris, a most severe lecture. But the appearance of this venerable man, as his friend, had the effect which Hatfield expected; for the Duke sent to enquire if he was the man who married the natural daughter of Lord Robert Manners, and being satisfied as to the fact, dispatched a messenger with £200 and had him released.

In the year 1784 or 1785, his Grace of Rutland was appointed Lord Lieutenant of Ireland, and shortly after his arrival in Dublin, Hatfield made his appearance in that city. He, immediately on his landing, engaged a suite of rooms at an hotel in College-green, and represented himself as nearly allied to the Viceroy, but that he could not appear at the castle until his horses, servants, and carriages arrived, which he ordered, before leaving England, to be shipped at Liverpool. The easy and familiar manner in which he addressed the master of the hotel, perfectly satisfied him that he had a man of consequence in the house, and matters were arranged accordingly. This being adjusted, Hatfield soon found his way to Lucas's Coffee-house, a place where people of a certain rank generally frequented; and, it being a new scene, the Yorkshire park, the Rutlandshire estate, and the connection with the Rutland family, stood their ground very well for a month.

At the expiration of that term, the bill at the hotel amounted to sixty pounds and upwards. The landlord became importunate, and after expressing his astonishment at the non-arrival of Mr. Hatfield's domestics, &c., requested that he might be permitted to send in his bill. This did not in the least confuse Hatfield: he immediately told the master of the hotel that very fortunately his agent, who received the rents of his estates in the north of England, was then in Ireland, and held a public appointment; he lamented that his agent was not then in Dublin; but he had the pleasure to know his stay in the country would not exceed three days. This satisfied the landlord, and at the expiration of the three days, he called upon the gentleman, whose name Hatfield had given him, and presented the account. Here followed another scene of confusion and surprise. The supposed agent of the Yorkshire estate very frankly told the man who delivered the bill that he had no other knowledge of the person who sent him than what common report furnished him with, that his general character in London was that of a romantic simpleton, whose plausibilities had imposed on several people, and plunged himself into repeated difficulties.

The landlord retired highly thankful for the information, and immediately arrested his guest, who was lodged in the prison of the Marshalsea. Hatfield had scarcely seated himself in his new lodgings, when he visited the gaoler's wife in her apartment, and in a whisper requested her not to tell any person that she had in her custody a near relation of the then Viceroy. The woman, astonished at the discovery, immediately showed him into the best apartment in the prison, had a table provided, and she, her husband, and Hatfield, constantly dined together for nearly three weeks, in the utmost harmony and good humour.

During this time he had petitioned the Duke for another supply, who, apprehensive that the fellow might continue his impositions in Dublin, released him on condition of his immediately quitting Ireland ; and his Grace sent a servant, who conducted him on board the packet that sailed the next tide for Holyhead.

In 1792 he went to Scarborough, introduced himself to the acquaintance of several persons of distinction in that neighbourhood, and insinuated that he was, by the interest of the Duke of Rutland, soon to be one of the representatives in parliament for the town of Scarborough. After several weeks stay at the principal inn in Scarborough, his imposture was detected by his inability to pay the bill. Soon after his arrival in London he was arrested for this debt, and thrown into prison. He had been eight years and a half in confinement, when a Miss Nation, of Devonshire, to whom he had become known, paid his debts, took him from prison, and gave him her hand in marriage.

Soon after he was liberated, he had the good fortune to prevail with some highly respectable merchants in Devonshire, to take him into partnership with them ! and with a clergyman to accept his drafts to a large amount. He made upon this foundation a splendid appearance in London, and, before the general election, even proceeded to canvass the rotten borough of Queenborough. Suspicions in the meantime arose in regard to his character and the state of his fortune. He retired from the indignation of his creditors, and was declared a bankrupt in order to bring his villainies to light. Thus, having left behind his second wife and two infant children at Tiverton, he visited other places; and, at length, in July, 1802, arrived at the Queen's Head, now the Queen's Hotel, in Keswick, in a handsome and well-appointed travelling carriage, but without any servant, where he assumed the name of the Honourable Alexander Augustus Hope, brother of the Earl of Hopetoun, and member for Linlithgow. From Keswick, as his head quarters, he made excursions in every direction amongst the neighbouring valleys ; meeting generally a good deal of respect and attention, partly on account of his handsome equipage, and still more from his visiting cards, which designated him as "The Honourable Alexander Augustus Hope." Some persons had discernment enough to doubt this: for his breeding and deportment, though showy, had a tinge of vulgarity about it ; he was grossly ungrammatical in his ordinary conversation. He received letters under this assumed name—*that* might be through collusion with accomplices—but he himself continually *franked* letters by that name. Now, *that* being a capital offence, being not only a forgery, but (as a forgery on the post-office), sure to be prosecuted, nobody presumed to question his pretensions any longer; and, henceforward, he went to all places with the consideration attached to an earl's brother. All doors flew open at his approach; boats, boatmen, nets, and the most unlimited sporting privileges, were placed at the disposal of the "Honourable" gentleman; and the hospitality of the whole country taxed itself to offer a suitable reception to the patrician Scotsman.

Nine miles from Keswick, by the nearest route, lies the lake of Buttermere. Its margin, which is overhung by some of the loftiest and steepest of Cumbrian mountains, exhibited on either side few traces of human neighbourhood; the level area, where the hills recede enough to allow of any, is of a wild pastoral character, or almost savage; the waters of the lake are deep and sullen; and the mountain barriers, by excluding the sun from much of its daily course, strengthen the gloomy impressions. At the foot of this lake (that is at the end where its waters issue), lie a few unornamented fields, through which rolls a little brook-like river, connecting it with the larger lake of Crummock, and at the edge of this little domain, upon the roadside, stands a cluster of cottages, so small and few, that, in the richer tracts of the islands, they would scarcely be complimented with the name of hamlet. One of these, the principal, belonged to an independent proprietor, called in the local dialect a "'Statesman;" and more, perhaps, for the sake of gathering any little local news, than with much view to pecuniary profit at that era, this cottage offered the accommodations of an inn to traveller and his horse. Rare, however, must have been the mounted traveller in those days, unless visiting Buttermere for itself, for the road led to no further habitations of man, with the exception of one or two pastoral cabins, equally humble, in Gatesgarth, situated at the head of Buttermere lake.

Hither, however, in an evil hour for the peace of this little brotherhood of shepherds, came the cruel spoiler from Keswick, and directed his steps to the once happy cottage of poor Mary, the daughter of Mr. and Mrs. Robinson, an old couple, who kept the Fish inn, and had by their industry gained a little property. She was their only daughter, and probably her name had never been known to the public, but for the account given of her by the author of " A Fortnight's Ramble to the Lakes in Westmorland, Lancashire, and Cumberland." His errand was to witness or share in char-fishing : for in Derwentwater (the lake at Keswick) no char is found, which breeds only in deep waters, such as Windermere, Crummock, Buttermere, &c. He now became acquainted with an Irish gentleman, and member of the then Irish parliament, who had been resident with his family some months at Keswick. With this gentleman, and under his immediate protection, there was likewise a young lady of family and fortune, and of great personal attractions. One o. the means which Hatfield used to introduce himself to this respectable family was the following : Under standing that the gentleman had been a military man, he took an army list from his pocket, and pointed to his assumed name, the Honourable Alexander Augustus Hope, lieutenant-colonel of the 14th regiment of foot. This new acquaintance daily gained strength ; and he shortly paid his addresses to the fair ward of the above gentleman, and obtained her consent. The wedding clothes were bought ; but previous to the wedding-day being fixed, she insisted that the pretended Colonel Hope should introduce the subject formally to her friends. He now pretended to write letters, and while waiting for the answers, proposed to employ that time in a trip to Lord Hopetoun's seat, &c.

From this time he played a double game ; his visits to Keswick became frequent, and his suit to the young lady assiduous and fervent. Still, however, both at

Keswick and Buttermere, he was somewhat shy of appearing in public. He was sure to be engaged in a fishing expedition on the day on which any company was expected at the public-house at Buttermere; and he never attended the church at Keswick but once.

Finding his schemes baffled to obtain this young lady and her fortune, he now applied himself wholly to gain possession of Mary Robinson, who was a fine young woman of eighteen, and acted in the capacity of waiter. In a situation so solitary, the stranger had unlimited facilities for enjoying her company, and recommending himself to her favour. Among the neighbours he made the most minute enquires into every circumstance relating to her and her family. Doubts about his pretensions never arose in so retired a place as this; they were over-ruled before they could well have arisen, by the opinion now general in Keswick, that he really was what he pretended to be: and thus with little demur, except in the shape of a few natural words of departing anger from a defeated or rejected rustic admirer, the young woman gave her hand in marriage to the showy and unprincipled stranger. He, in company with the clergyman, procured a license on the 1st of October, and they were publicly married in the church of Lorton, on Saturday the 2nd of October, 1802. A romantic account of it found its way almost immediately into the newspapers. It thus fell under the notice of various individuals in Scotland, who knew that Colonel Hope, who was said to have married the Flower of Buttermere, had been abroad the whole summer, and was now residing in Vienna. Mr. Charles Hope, then Lord Justice Clerk, afterwards president of the Court of Session (a son-in-law of the Earl of Hopetoun), had, it is believed, a chief share in making this fact known, and promoting the enquiries which led to the detection of the imposture.

On the day previous to his marriage, he wrote to

Mr. N. M. More, informing him that he was under the necessity of being absent for ten days on a journey into Scotland, and sent him a draft for thirty pounds, drawn on Mr. Crump, of Liverpool, desired him to cash it, and pay some small debts in Keswick with it, and send him over the balance, as he feared he might be short of cash on the road. This Mr. More immediately did, and sent him ten guineas in addition to the balance. On the Saturday, Mr. Wood, the landlord of the Queen's Head, returned from Lorton with the intelligence that Colonel Hope had married the Beauty of Buttermere. As it was clear, whoever he was, that he had acted unworthily and dishonourably, Mr. More's suspicions were of course awakened. He instantly remitted the draft to Mr. Crump, who immediately accepted it. As the friend of the young lady, whom he (Hatfield) first paid his addresses to, he wrote to the Earl of Hopetoun. Before the answer arrived, the pretended honourable returned with his wife to Buttermere. He went only as far as Longtown, when he received two letters, seemed much troubled that some friends whom he had expected had not arrived there, stayed three days, and then told his wife that he would go back again to Buttermere. From this she was seized with fears and suspicions. They returned, however, and their return was made known at Keswick. The late Mr. Harding, the barrister, and a Welch judge, a very singular man, passing through Keswick, heard of this imposter, and sent his servant over to Buttermere with a note to the supposed Colonel Hope, who observed, " that it was a mistake, and that it was for a brother of his." However, he sent for four horses, and came over to Keswick: drew another draft upon Mr. Crump, for twenty pounds, which the landlord of the Queen's Head had the courage to cash. Of this sum he immediately sent the ten guineas to Mr. More, who came and introduced him to the judge as his old friend Colonel Hope. But he made a blank denial that he had ever assumed the name. He had said that his name was Hope, but not that he was the honourable member for Linlithgow, &c., &c.; and one who had been his frequent intimate at Buttermere gave evidence to the same purpose.

In spite, however, of his impudent assertions, and those of his associate, the evidence against him was decisive. A warrant was issued by Sir Frederick Vane, of Armathwaite Hall, Basenthwaite Lake, on the clear proof of his having forged and received several franks as the member for Linlithgow, and he was committed to the care of a constable, but allowed to fish on the lake. Having, however, found means to escape, he was conducted by a guide belonging to Keswick, named Edward Birkett, through the vale of Borrowdale, over the pass of Sty-head to Wastdale, and thence to Ravenglass, where he took refuge and lay concealed for a few days on board a sloop, and then went in the coach to Ulverston, and was afterwards seen at an hotel in Chester. In the meantime the following advertisement, setting forth his person and manners, appeared in the papers :—

"NOTORIOUS IMPOSTOR, SWINDLER, AND FELON!

"John Hatfield, who lately married a young woman, commonly called the Beauty of Buttermere, under an assumed name; height about five feet ten inches, aged about forty-four, full face, bright eyes, thick eye brows; strong, but light beard, good complexion, with some colour; thick, but not very prominent nose, smiling countenance, fine teeth, a scar on one of his cheeks near the chin, very long thick light hair, and a great deal of it grey done up in a club; stiff square shouldered, full breast and chest, rather corpulent, and strong limbed, but very active; and has rather a spring in his gait, with apparently a little hitch in bringing up one leg; the two middle fingers of his left hand are stiff from an old wound; he has something of the Irish brogue in his speech; fluent and elegant in his language, great command of words, frequently puts his hand to his heart; very fond of compliments, and generally addressing himself to persons most distinguished by rank and situation; attentive in the extreme to females, and likely to insinuate himself where there are young ladies. He was in America during the war; is fond of talking of his wounds and exploits there, and of military subjects, as well as Hatfield Hall, and his estates in Derbyshire and Cheshire; and of the antiquity of his family, whom he pretends to trace to the Plantagenets. He makes a boast of having often been engaged in duels; he has been a great traveller also, by his own account, and talks of Egypt, Turkey, and Italy; and in short has a general knowledge of subjects, which, together with his engaging manners, is well calculated to impose upon the credulous. He had art enough to connect himself with some very respectable merchants in Devonshire, as a partner in business, but having swindled them out of large sums, he was made a separate bankrupt in June, 1802. He cloaks his deception under the mask of religion, appears fond of religious conversation, and makes a point of attending divine service and popular preachers."

Besides blighting the prospects of the poor girl, he had nearly ruined her father by running up a debt of eighteen pounds. His dressing case, a very elegant piece of furniture, was left behind, and on being opened at Keswick by warrant of a magistrate, was found to contain every article that the most luxurious gentleman could desire, but no papers tending to discover his real name. Afterwards, Mary herself, searching more narrowly, discovered that the box had a double bottom, and in the intermediate recess found a number of letters addressed to him by his *wife and children*, under the name of Hatfield. The story of the detection immediately became as notorious as the marriage had been.

Though he was personally known in Chester to many of the inhabitants, yet this specious hypocrite had so artfully disguised himself, that he quitted the town without any suspicions before the Bow-street officers reached that place in quest of him. He was then traced to Brielth in Brecknockshire, and was at length apprehended about sixteen miles from Swansea, and committed to Brecon gaol. He had a cravat on with his initials, J. H., which he attempted to account for by calling himself John Henry,

Before the magistrates he declared himself to be Ludor Henry; and in order to prepossess the honest Cambrians in his favour, boasted that he was descended from an ancient family in Wales, for the inhabitants of which country he had ever entertained a sincere regard. He was, however, conveyed up to town by the Bow-street officers, where he was examined on his arrival before the magistrates. The solicitor for his bankruptcy attended to identify his person, and stated that the commission of bankruptcy was issued against Hatfield in June, 1802; that he attended the last meeting of the commissioners, but the prisoner did not appear, although due notice had been given in the Gazette, and he himself had given notice to the prisoner's wife, at Wakefield, near Tiverton, Devon. Mr. Parkyn, the solicitor to the post-office, produced a warrant from Sir Frederick Vane, bart., a magistrate for the county of Cumberland, against the prisoner, by the name of the Hon. Alexander Augustus Hope, charging him with felony, by pretending to be a member of Parliament of the United Kingdom, and franking several letters by the name of A. Hope, to several persons, which were put into the post-office at Keswick, in Cumberland, in order to evade the duties of postage. Another charge of forgery, and the charge for bigamy, were explained to him, but not entered into, as he was committed for trial on these charges to the next assizes at Carlisle. He conducted himself with the greatest propriety during his journey to town, and on his examinations; but said nothing more than answering a few questions put to him by Sir Richard Ford and the solicitors, affecting to consider himself a persecuted individual, and representing in particular, that, in the alliance with Mary Robinson, he had been rather sinned against than sinning. Mary, on the other hand, who was now announced to be likely to bear a child to her pretended husband, refused to become accessory to his prosecution. The utmost she could be prevailed on to do against Hatfield was to address the following letter to Sir Richard Ford:—

"The man whom I had the misfortune to marry, and who has ruined me and my aged parents, always told me he was the Hon. Colonel Hope, the next brother of the Earl of Hopetoun.
Your grateful and unfortunate servant,
MARY ROBINSON."

At the fourth examination of the impostor, on the 27th of December, this letter was read aloud by the clerk, in the open court. To quote from a chronicle of the time—"The simplicity of this letter, which, though it breathes the soft murmur of complaint, is free from all virulence, excited in the breast of every person present an emotion of pity and respect for the unmerited sorrows of a female, who has in this whole matter manifested a delicacy of sentiment and nobleness of mind infinitely beyond her sphere of education. The feelings of Hatfield could not be enviable; yet he exhibited no symptom of contrition, and when remanded for further examination, retired with the most impenetrable composure."

He was then dressed in a black coat and waistcoat, fustian breeches, and boots, and wore his hair tied behind without powder. His appearance was respectable, though quite *en deshabille*. The Duke of Cumberland, and several other gentlemen, were present at his examination, in the course of which the following letter was produced:—

Buttermere, Oct. 1, 1802.
Dear Sir,
"I have this day received Mr. Firkman's kind letter from Manchester, promising me the happiness of seeing you both in about ten days, which will indeed give me great pleasure; and you can, too, be of very valuable service to me at this place, particulars of which when we meet, though I shall probably write to you again in a few days—the chief purpose for which I write this is to desire you will be so good as to accept a bill for me, dated Buttermere, the 1st of October, at ten days, and I will either give you cash for it here, or remit to you in time

which ever way you please to say. It is drawn in favour of Nathaniel Montgomery More, Esq. Be pleased to present my best respects to your lady; and say I hope, ere the winter elapses, to pay her my personal respects; for if you will manage so as to pass a little time with me in Scotland, I will promise to make Liverpool in my way to London.

"With the truest esteem,
"I am, dear sir, yours ever,
"A. HOPE."

"Keswick, October the 1st, 1802.
John Crumpt, Esq. Liverpool.
Free, A. Hope."

This letter, it was proved, passed free of postage. Another letter was also produced from his wife at Tiverton, and a certificate of his marriage with Mary of Buttermere. His trial came on August 15th, 1803, at the Assizes for Cumberland, before the Honourable Alexander Thompson, Knt. He stood charged upon the three following indictments:

1. With having assumed the name and title of the Honourable Alexander Augustus Hope, and pretending to be a member of parliament of the United Kingdom of Great Britain and Ireland, and with having, about the month of October last, under such false and fictitious name and character, drawn a draft or bill of exchange, in the name of Alexander Hope, upon John Crumpt, Esq., for the sum of £20, payable to George Wood, of Keswick, Cumberland, innkeeper, or order, at the end of fourteen days from the date of the said draft or bill of exchange.

2. With making, uttering, and publishing as true, a certain false, forged, and counterfeit bill of exchange, with the name of Alexander Augustus Hope thereunto falsely set and subscribed, drawn upon John Crumpt, Esq., dated the 1st of October, 1802, and payable to Nathaniel Montgomery More, or order, ten days after date, for £30 sterling.

3. With having assumed the name of Alexander Hope, and pretending to be a member of parliament of the United Kingdom of Great Britain and Ireland,

the brother of the right Hon. Lord Hopetoun, and a Colonel in the army; and under such false and fictitious name and character, at various times in the month of October, 1802, having forged and counterfeited the hand-writing of the said Alexander Hope, in the superscription of certain letters or packets, in order to avoid the payment of the duty on postage.

The prisoner pleaded not guilty to these charges.

The three several indictments having been read, Mr. Scarlett, afterwards Lord Abinger, opened the case in an address to the jury, and gave an ample detail of the prisoner's guilt.

In support of what he had advanced, he called Mr. Quick, who was clerk in the house at Tiverton where Hatfield was partner, who swore to his hand-writing.

The Rev. Mr. Nicholson swore that when the prisoner was asked his name, he said it was a most comfortable one, Hope. The other witnesses were Mr. Joseph Skelton, of Rockliffe, Cumberland; Mr. George Wood, of Keswick, innkeeper; John Gregory Crumpt, and Colonel Parke, who were well acquainted with the real Colonel Hope.

The evidence for the prosecution having closed, the prisoner then addressed himself to the jury. He said he felt some degree of satisfaction in being able to have his sufferings terminated, as they must of course be by their verdict. For the space of nine months he had been dragged from prison to prison, and torn from place to place, subject to all the misrepresentations of calumny. " Whatever will be my fate," said he," I am content; it is the award of justice, impartially and virtuously administered. But I will solemnly declare, that in all my transactions, I never intended to defraud or injure the persons whose names have appeared in the prosecution. This I will maintain to the last of my life."

The prisoner called in his defence ———Newton, attorney at Chester; who said he was employed by

C

the prisoner at the summer assizes in recovering an estate in the county of Kent. He understood the prisoner's father to be a respectable man; some of the family very opulent. Believes the prisoner has a mother-in-law; says the prisoner is married; never knew him to bear any other name than John Hatfield; he married a lady of the name of Nation. His assignees have sold the estate in question. Witness knows nothing of his circumstances previous to the recovery of the estate. It was rented at £100 per annum. Does not know why the prisoner quitted Devonshire. Did not then travel in his own carriage, but formerly kept a carriage.

After the evidence was gone through, his lordship, Sir A. Thompson, with a great deal of perspicuity and force, summed up the whole of the evidence, and commented upon such parts as peculiarly affected the fate of the prisoner. "Nothing," his lordship said, "could be more clearly proved, than that the prisoner did make the bill or bills in question under the assumed name of Alexander Augustus Hope, with an intention to defraud. That the prisoner used the additional name of Augustus was of no consequence in this question. The evidence proved clearly that the prisoner meant to represent himself to be another character; and under that assumed character, he drew the bills in question. If anything should appear in mitigation of the offences with which the prisoner was charged, they must give them a full consideration; and though his character had been long shaded with obloquy, yet they must not let this in the least influence the verdict they were sworn to give."

The jury consulted about ten minutes, and then returned a verdict—*Guilty of Forgery*.

The trial commenced about eleven o'clock in the forenoon, and ended about seven in the evening, during the whole o which time the court was excessively crowded. The prisoner's behaviour in court was proper and dignified, and he supported his situation from first to last with unshaken fortitude. He employed himself during the greatest part of his trial in writing notes on the evidence given, and in conversing with his counsel, Messrs. Topping and Holroyd.

When the verdict of the jury was given, he manifested no relaxation of his accustomed demeanour. After the court adjourned, he retired from the bar, and was ordered to attend the next morning to receive the sentence of the law. The crowd was immense, and he was allowed a post-chaise from the town-hall to the gaol.*

At eight o'clock the next morning the court met again, when the prisoner appeared at the bar to receive his sentence. Numbers of people gathered together to witness this painful duty of the law passed upon one whose appearance, manners, and actions, had excited a most uncommon degree of interest. After proceeding in the usual form, the judge addressed the prisoner in the following impressive terms:

"John Hatfield, after the long and serious investigation of the charges which have been preferred against you, you have been found guilty by a jury of your country.

"You have been distinguished for crimes of such magnitude as have seldom, if ever, received any mitigation of capital punishment; and in your case it is impossible it can be limited. Assuming the person, name, and character of a worthy and respectable officer, a member of a noble family in this country, you have perpetrated and committed the most enormous crimes. The long imprisonment you have undergone has afforded time for your serious reflection, and an

---

*The gaol and court-house were at that period divided by the street. The gaol, &c., has since been rebuilt, and there is now a passage from one to the other.

opportunity of your being deeply impressed with a sense of the enormity of your crimes, and the justness of that sentence which must be inflicted upon you; and I wish you to be seriously impressed with the awfulness of your situation. I conjure you to reflect with anxious care and deep concern on your approaching end, concerning which much remains to be done. Lay aside now your delusions and impositions, and employ properly the short space you have to live. I beseech you to employ the remaining part of your time in preparing for eternity, so that you may find mercy at the hour of death, and in the day of judgment. Hear now the sentence of the law:—That you be carried from hence to the place from whence you came, and from thence to the place of execution, and there to be hung by the neck till you are dead: and may the Lord have mercy on your soul!"

A notion very generally prevailed that he would not be brought to justice, and the arrival of the mail was daily expected with the greatest impatience. No pardon arriving, Saturday, September 3rd, 1803, was at last fixed upon for the execution.

The gallows was erected the preceding night between twelve and three, on an island formed by the river Eden, on the north side of the town, between the two bridges. From the hour when the jury found him guilty he behaved with the utmost serenity and cheerfulness. He talked upon the topics of the day, with the greatest interest or indifference. He could scarcely ever be brought to speak of his own case. He neither blamed the verdict, nor made any confession of his guilt. He said he had no intention to defraud those whose names he forged; but was never heard to say that he was to die unjustly. None of his relations ever visited him during his confinement.

The alarming nature of the crime of forgery, in a commercial country, had taught him from the beginning to entertain no hope of mercy. By ten in the morning of September 3 his irons were struck off; he appeared as usual, and no one observed any alteration or increased agitation whatever.

Soon after ten o'clock he sent for the *Carlisle Journal*, and perused it for some time. A little after he had laid aside the paper, two clergymen (Mr. Pattison of Carlisle, and Mr. Mark of Burgh-on-Sands), attended and prayed with him for about two hours, and drank coffee with him. After they left him, about twelve, he wrote some letters, and in one he enclosed his penknife; it was addressed to London. About this time he also shaved himself; though entrusted with a razor, he never seems to have meditated an attempt upon his life; but it was generally reported on Friday night that he had poisoned himself, though without any foundation. To all who spoke with him, he pretended that what he had to suffer was a matter of little consequence. He preferred talking on indifferent subjects. At three, he dined with the gaoler, and ate heartily. Having taken a glass or two of wine, he ordered coffee. He took a cup a few minutes before he set out for the place of execution. The last thing he did was to read a chapter from the 2d Corinthians. He had previously marked out this passage for his lesson before he was to mount the scaffold.

The sheriffs, the bailiffs, and the Carlisle volunteer cavalry, attended at the gaol door about half-past three, together with a post-chaise and hearse. He was then ordered into the turnkey's lodge, for the purpose of being pinioned, where he inquired of the gaoler, who were going in the chaise with him? He was told, the executioner and the gaoler. He immediately said, " Pray, where is the executioner? I should wish much to see him." The executioner was sent for. Hatfield asked him how he was, and made him a present of some silver in a paper. During the time of his being pinioned, he stood with resolution, and requested he might not be pinioned tight, as he wished to use his handkerchief on the platform ; which request was complied with. A prodigious crowd had assembled; this being market-day, numbers of people had come from a distance of many miles, out of mere curiosity, to witness the execution. Hatfield, when he left the prison, wished all his fellow prisoners might be happy : he then took a farewell of the clergyman, who attended him to the door of the chaise, and mounted its steps with much steadiness and composure. The gaoler and executioner went in along with him. The latter had been brought from Dumfries upon a retaining fee of ten guineas.

It was exactly four o'clock when the procession moved from the gaol. Passing through the Scotch gate, in about twelve minutes it arrived at the Sands. Half the yeomanry went before the carriage, and the other half behind. Upon arriving on the ground, they formed a ring round the scaffold. It is said that he wished to have the blinds drawn up, but that such an indulgence was held inconsistent with the interest of public justice. When he came in sight of the gallows, he said to the gaoler, he imagined that was the tree (pointing to it) that he was to die on. On being told that it was, he exclaimed, "Oh ! a happy sight—I see it with pleasure !"

As soon as the carriage door had been opened by the under-sheriff, he alighted with his two companions. A small dung cart, boarded over, had been placed under the gibbet, and a ladder was placed against it, which he instantly ascended. He was dressed in a black jacket, black silk waistcoat, fustian pantaloons, shoes, and white cotton stockings. He was perfectly cool and collected. At the same time, his conduct displayed nothing of levity, of insensibility, or of hardihood. He was more anxious to give proof of resignation than of heroism. His countenance was extremely pale, but his hand never trembled. He immediately untied his neckerchief, and placed a bandage over his eyes. Then he desired the hangman, who was extremely awkward, to be as expert as possible about it, and that he would wave a handkerchief when he was ready. The executioner not having fixed the rope in its proper place, he put up his hand and turned it himself. He tied his cap and his neckerchief about his head also. Then he requested the gaoler would step on the platform and pinion his arms a little harder, saying, that when he had lost his senses he might attempt to lift them to his neck. The rope was completely fixed about five minutes before five o'clock: it was slack, and he merely said, "May the Almighty bless you all." Nor did he falter in the least, when he tied the cap, shifted the rope, and took his neckerchief from his neck.

He several times put on a languid and piteous smile. He at last seemed rather exhausted and faint. Having been near three weeks under sentence of death, he must have suffered much, nothwithstanding his external bearing; and a reflection of the misery he had occasioned must have given him many an agonizing throb.

Having taken leave of the gaoler and sheriff, he prepared himself for his fate. He was at this time heard to exclaim, "My spirit is strong, though my body is weak."

Great apprehensions were entertained that it would be necessary to tie him up a second time. The noose slipped twice, and he fell down about eighteen inches. His feet at last were almost touching the ground, but his excessive weight, which occasioned this accident, speedily relieved him from pain. He expired in a moment, and without any struggle. The ceremony of his hands being tied behind his back, was satisfied by a piece of white tape passed loosely from one to the other, but he never made the slightest effort to relieve himself. He had calculated so well, that his money lasted exactly to the scaffold. As they were setting out, the executioner was going to search him. He threw him half-a-crown, saying, " This is all my pockets contain." He had been in considerable distress before he received a supply from his father. He afterwards lived in great style, frequently making presents to his fellow felons. He was considered in the gaol as a kind of emperor : he was allowed to do whatever he pleased, and no one took offence at the air of superiority which he assumed.

He was cut down after he had hung about an hour. On the preceding Wednesday he had applied to one of the clergymen who attended him (Mr. Pattison) to recommend him a tradesman to make his coffin. Mr. Joseph Bushby, of Carlisle, took measure of him. He did not appear at all agitated while Mr. Bushby was so employed ; but told him that he wished the coffin to be a strong oak one, plain and neat. " I request, Sir," he added, " that after I am taken down, I may be put into the coffin immediately, with the apparel I may have on, and afterwards tightly screwed down, put into the hearse which will be in waiting, carried to the churchyard of Burgh-on-Sands, and there be interred in the evening."

The coffin, which was made of oak, was, however, adorned with plates, and extremely handsome every way. A hearse, which was in waiting according to his orders, followed with it to the ground, and afterwards bore him away. It seems he had a great terror of his body being taken up ; and though he was told that it would be safer for him to be buried in the city, yet he preferred Burgh, a place extremely sequestered, about five miles west from Carlisle ; but the conscientious parishioners of place objected to his being laid there, and the body was consequently conveyed in the hearse to St. Mary's churchyard, Carlisle, close by the northern gate, the usual place for those who come to an untimely end. Several men then set to work to dig a grave. The spot fixed upon was in a distant corner of the churchyard, far from the other tombs. No priest attended, and the coffin was lowered without any religious service. Notwithstanding his varied and complicated enormities, his untimely end excited considerable commiseration in this place. His manners were extremely polished and insinuating, and he was possessed of qualities which might have rendered him an ornament to society.

The following is a copy of Hatfield's Epitaph.

"OUR LIFE IS BUT A WINTER'S DAY,
SOME ONLY BREAKFAST AND AWAY;
OTHERS TO DINNER STAY,
AND ARE FULL FED;
THE OLDEST MAN BUT SUPS AND GOES TO BED.
LARGE IS HIS DEBT WHO LINGERS OUT HIS DAY;
HE WHO GOES THE SOONEST HAS THE LEAST TO PAY."

The unfortunate Mary of Buttermere, for a time, went from home to avoid the impertinent visits of unfeeling curiosity. By all accounts she was much affected; and, indeed, without supposing that any part of her former attachment remained, it is impossible that she could view his tragical fate with indifference. When her father and mother heard that Hatfield had certainly been executed, they both exclaimed, "God be thanked!"

On the day of his condemnation, Wordsworth and Coleridge passed through Carlisle, and endeavoured to obtain an interview with him. Wordsworth succeeded; but, for some unknown reason, the prisoner steadily refused to see Coleridge; a caprice which could not be penetrated. It was true that he had, during his whole residence at Keswick, avoided Coleridge with a solicitude which had revived the original suspicions against him in some quarters, after they had generally subsided. However, if not him, Coleridge saw and examined his very interesting papers. These were chiefly letters from women whom he had injured, pretty much in the same way and by the same impostures as he had so recently practised in Cumberland. Great was the emotion of Coleridge when he afterwards recurred to these letters, and bitter—almost vindictive—was the indignation with which he spoke of Hatfield. One set of letters appeared to have been written under too certain a knowledge of *his* villainy towards the individual to whom they were addressed; though still relying on some possible remains of humanity, or perhaps (the poor writer might have thought) on some lingering relics of affection for herself. The other set was even more distressing; they were written under the first conflicts of suspicions, alternately repelling with warmth the gloomy doubts which were fast arising, and then yielding to their afflicting evidence; raving in one page under the misery of alarm, in another courting the delusions of hope, and luring back the perfidious deserter—here resigning herself to despair, and there again labouring to show that all might yet be well. Coleridge said often " In looking back upon that frightful exposure of human guilt and misery, that the man who, when pursued by these heart-rending apostrophes, and with this litany of anguish sounding in his ears, from despairing women and famishing children, could yet find it possible to enjoy the calm pleasures of a lake tourist, and deliberately hunt for the picturesque, must have been a fiend of that order which, fortunately, does not often emerge amongst men." It is painful to remember that, in those days, amongst the multitude who ended their career in the same ignominious way, and the majority for offences connected with the forgery of bank notes, there must have been a considerable number who perished from the opposite cause,—namely, because they felt, too passionately and profoundly for prudence, the claims of those who looked up to them for support. One common scaffold confounds the most flinty hearts and the tenderest. However, in this instance it was in some measure the heartless part of Hatfield's conduct which drew upon him his ruin; for the Cumberland jury, it has been asserted, declared their unwillingness to hang him for having forged a frank; and both they, and those who refused to aid his escape, when first apprehended, were reconciled to this harshness entirely by what they heard of his conduct to their injured young fellow countrywoman.

Every year since, shoals of tourists have crowded to the secluded lake and the little homely cabaret (the Fish inn), which had been the scene of her brief romance. It was fortunate for a person in her distressing situation that her home was not in a town; the few and simple neighbours who had witnessed her imaginary elevation, having little knowledge of worldly feelings, never for an instant connected with her disappointment any sense of the ludicrous, or spoke of it as a calamity to which her vanity might have co-operated. They treated it as unmixed injury, reflecting shame on nobody but the wicked perpetrator.

"Hence," says De Quincey, "without much trial to her womanly sensibilities, she found herself able to resume her situation in the little inn. In that place and in that capacity I saw her, and shall here say a word upon her personal appearance, because the lake poets all admired her greatly. Her figure was good in my eye, but I doubt whether most of my readers would have thought so. She was none of your evanescent wasp-waisted beauties; on the contrary, she was rather large every way, tallish, and proportionately broad. Her face was fair, and her features feminine, and unquestionably she was what all the world would call 'good-looking,' except in her arms, which had something of a statuesque beauty, and in her carriage, which expressed a womanly grace.

I looked in vain for any positive qualities of any kind or degree :—beautiful in any emphatic sense she was not, everything about her face and bust was negative; simply without offence. Even this, however, was more than could be said at all times, for the expression could be disagreeable; this arose out of her situation, connected as it was with defective sensibility and a misdirected pride.

Nothing operates so differently upon different minds and different styles of beauty as the inquisitive gaze of strangers, whether in the spirit of respectful admiration or of insolence. In Mary of Buttermere it roused mere anger and disdain, which, meeting with the sense of her humble and dependent situation, gave birth to a most unhappy aspect of countenance. * * * Men who had no touch of a gentleman's nature in their composition sometimes insulted her by words and looks, supposing that they purchased the right to do so by an extra half-crown. Thus she too readily attributed the same spirit of impertinent curiosity to every man whose eyes happened to settle steadily upon her face. Yet once at least I must have seen her under the most favourable circumstances, for on my first visit to Buttermere I had the pleasure of Mr. Southey's* company, who was incapable of wounding anyone's feelings, and to Mary in particular was well known by kind attentions, and, I believe, by some service; then, at least, I saw her to some advantage, and perhaps for a figure of her build at the best age, for it was nine or ten years after her misfortune. We were a solitary pair of tourists, nothing arose to confuse or distress her. She waited upon us at dinner, and talked to us freely. She, meantime, under the

---

* Late Poet Laureate.

name of 'The Beauty of Buttermere,' became an object of interest to all England. Melodramas were produced in London theatres upon her story."

Mary was afterwards united to a respectable farmer, in another part of the county, and, unfortunately for her poetical fame, became "fat and well-looking," and without anything in her appearance which might lead to the discovery that she was a person who had at one time been the subject of the poet's song.

———o———

The following address to "Mary of Buttermere" is from

WORDSWORTH'S PRELUDE.

[The distant friend here apostrophised was the late S. T. Coleridge, then at Malta.]

> " Friend, O distant friend : a story drawn
> From our own ground—the Maid of Buttermere ;
> And how, unfaithful to a virtuous wife,
> Devoted and deceived, the spoiler came
> And woo'd the artless Daughter of the Hills,
> And wedded her in cursed mockery
> Of love and marriage bonds.
> These words to thee
> Must needs bring back the moment when we first,
> Ere the broad world rang with the maiden's name,
> Beheld her serving at the cottage inn ;
> Both stricken, as she entered or withdrew,
> With admiration of her modest mien
> And carriage, marked by unexampled grace.
> We, since that time, not unfamiliarly
> Have seen her—her discretion have observed,
> Her just opinions, delicate reserve,
> Her patience and humility of mind,

Unspoiled by commendation and the excess
Of public notice—an offensive light
To a meek spirit suffering inwardly."

"It should be added that William Wordsworth and Samuel Taylor Coleridge had seen Mary more frequently and conversed with her much more than myself.—Truly yours, R. SOUTHEY."

BUTTERMERE & PENNY POSTAGE.

Sir Rowland Hill's death, in 1879, recalls an incident which fell under his notice more than forty years before, and which he repeated to a committee of the House of Commons in proof of his statement that the then high postal charges upon letters were not only all but prohibitory but were also a cause of demoralization among the people, as training them in habits of deceit and evasion. Hill was recruiting himself among the Cumberland fells, and was lodged near Buttermere Lake. One morning, hearing the postman's horn, he walked down to the wicket and got his letters. Behind him was the servant of the house, and to her the postman said, "Here's yan for thee, Matty." "Let's see't," said Matty, who, taking it, gave a glance at the address, and handed it back with a fine air of mixed indignation and astonishment, exclaiming, "Pay saxpence! I'll du nowt o' t' swort; tak it wid thee." The postman replied, "Varra weel, suit thy sel'," and walked away.

Hill, who was standing by, fancied that poverty might have prompted the girl's refusal, and willing to assist, questioned her and got for answer, "O it's a' reet, the letter's frae my brudder Ben. He's at sarvice, nigh Peerith, an' we 'greed when he left that he'd reet an' say if he'd be hyame at Martimas. If he cood na get, he'd pit a cross on t' left haun corner; an' if he could get, he'd pit yan on t' reet haun. A got a leuk o' t' letter, en' Ben'll be here at Martimas." And Matty went singing away.

CUMBERLAND LASSES AT THE ROYAL AGRICULTURAL SOCIETY'S SHOW AT CARLISLE, 1880.

The "Man of Mark Lane," in his notes on the great show at Carlisle, which, like the Kilburn one of the previous year, was spoiled by the heavy rains, writes —"It was a subject of common remark in the showyard that the Cumberland lasses came dressed in the most sensible manner to suit a showyard on a wet day of any lady showgoers that the speakers had seen. There were no low shoes and worked stockings, as there were at Kilburn, and scarcely any gay dresses or elaborate white skirts. Almost, without exception, these sensible lasses came clad in waterproofs down to their ankles, and with little finery to be spoilt by any amount of rain. Altogether they looked the kind of farmers' wives and daughters to face agricultural depression, either by stopping here or going into the distant parts of the earth to get a living. I fancy some of them could give Mrs. Davison and the other members of the Lady-Farmers' Club a wrinkle or two. Let me not be misunderstood. Although, like Jenny Wren, these Cumberland lasses had put on their "brown gowns," and had not dressed "too fine," and although they looked as if they could face depression, they were not by any means deficient in attractions—not at all maid-of-all-work looking lasses. On the contrary, I have never seen—but no, I will not go on; these columns are sometimes read at my own house, and perhaps a little caution in a matter of this kind is desirable. The men of Cumberland (here I am on safe ground) are noted as athletes, and are a fine looking set of fellows; but they are certainly not superior to their wives and daughters."

THRELKELD HALL AND THE CASTLE ROCK, VALE OF ST. JOHN'S.

About four miles east of Keswick, is Threlkeld Hall, now a dilapidated farmhouse, but with a high romance associated with it. Here was brought up in humble but safe seclusion, the young Clifford, son of that worthless noble who slew the young Earl of Rutland, and, therefore, for whose innocent blood the swords of York were all athirst:

> "There at Blencathra's rugged feet,
> Sir Lancelot gave a safe retreat
> To noble Clifford,—from annoy
> Concealed the persecuted boy."

He dwelt as a shepherd here for four-and-twenty years, without learning even so much as to read and write, but leading, as it seems, a very contented life, under the protection of Sir Lancelot Threlkeld, who had married his mother, and behaved to him with a generosity very unusual with stepfathers of that period. On the succession of Henry VII., he was restored to his estates; and conducted himself in such a manner as to exchange the title of "The Shepherd Lord" for that of "The good Lord Clifford."

> "In him the savage virtues of his race,
> Revenge and all ferocious thoughts, were dead;
> Nor did he change; but keep in lofty place
> The wisdom which adversity had bred."

The valley of St. John runs directly southward from Threlkeld, and in front is the famed Castle Rock, apparently barring the defile. The greatest of British descriptive poets has thus described it in his *Bridal of Triermain:*—

> "Paled in by many a lofty hill,
> The narrow dale lay smooth and still;
> And, down its verdant bosom led,
> A winding brooklet found its bed."

In Bowscale Tarn, on Saddleback, tradition asserts that two immortal fish have their abode. The homage of these fish is amongst the acknowledgments which are stated by the Minstrel, in his " Song at the feast of Brougham Castle," to have been paid to the secret power of the good Lord Clifford, when a shepherd-boy, in adversity—

> "And both the undying fish that swim
> In Bowscale Tarn, did wait on him;
> The pair were servants of his eye
> In their immortality;
> They moved about in open sight,
> To and fro, for his delight."

THRELKELD TARN.

Exaggerating travellers have described Threlkeld Tarn as an abyss of waters upon which the sun never shines, and wherein the stars of heaven may be seen at noonday. Sir Walter Scott alludes to this fable in these lines of the Bridal of Triermain :—

> "Above her solitary track
> Rose Blencathra's ridgy back,
> Amid whose yawning gulfs the sun
> Cast umber'd raidance red and dim:
> Though never sun-beam could discern
> The surface of that sable tarn,
> In whose black mirror you may spy
> The stars while noon-tide lights the sky."

A THOUGHT SUGGESTED BY A VIEW OF SADDLEBACK.
By S. T. Coleridge.

> "On stern Blencathra's perilous height
> The winds are tyrannous and strong;
> And flashing forth unsteady light,
> From stern Blencathra's skyey height,
> How loud the torrents throng!
> Beneath the moon in gentle weather,
> They bind the earth and sky together;
> But oh! the sky and all its forms how quiet,
> The things that seek the earth, how full of noise and riot!"

SKIDDAW, KESWICK.

* * * * * * * * * *

"'Whea that hes climb'd Skiddaw hes seen sec a prospec,
　Where fells frown owre fells and in majesty vie?
Whea that hes seen Keswick can count hauf its beauties,
　May e'en try to count hauf the stars i' the sky;
Theer's Ullswater, Bassenthwaite, Wastwater, Derwent,
　That thousands on thousands ha'e travelled to view;
The langer they gaze still the mair they may wonder,
　And ay as they wonder may fin' summet new."

* * * * * * * * * *

" I stopp'd on a fell, tuik a lang luik at Skiddaw."

* * * * * * * * * *

Anderson.

The wonderful panoramic views from Skiddaw are eulogised by the enraptured Poet, Wordsworth, in a fine sonnet :—

" Pelion and Ossa flourish side by side,
　Together in immortal books enrolled;
His ancient dower Olympus hath not sold,
　And that aspiring hill, which did divide
Into two ample horns his forehead wide,
　Shines with poetic radiance as of old;
While not an English mountain we behold
　By the celestial muses glorified.
Yet round our sea-girt shore they rise in crowds,
　What was the great Parnassus' self to thee,
Mount Skiddaw? In its natural sovereignty,
　Our British hill is nobler far, he shrouds
His double front among Atlantic clouds,
　And pours forth streams more sweet than Castaly.'

Even the city-loving Elia (Charles Lamb) was enraptured with Skiddaw and its views. " O! its fine black head," he writes in one of his letters, " and the bleak air a-top of it, with a prospect of mountains all about and about, making you giddy; and then Scotland afar off, and the border counties so famous in song and ballad! It was a day that will stand out like a mountain, I am sure, in my life." " Bleak " the air is, indeed, "atop," exposed, as the summit is, to the sea-winds. Michael Drayton alludes in one of his poems to

"Snow-crowned Skiddaw's lofty cliffs,"

and a poet of later years, John Keats, compares an earnest gazer to one who would—

" From off old Skiddaw's top, when fog conceals
His rugged forehead in a mantle pale,
With an eye guess towards some pleasant vale,
Descry a favourite hamlet faint and fair."

YEW TREES.

Near the celebrated black-lead mine in Borrowdale is the little less celebrated yew trees to be seen, of which Wordsworth says :—

" Those fraternal four of Borrowdale,
Joined in one solemn and capacious grove
Huge trunks, and each particular trunk a growth
Of intertwisted fibres, serpentine,
Up-coiling, and inveterately convolved :
Nor uninformed with phantasy, and looks
That threaten the profane ;—a pillared shade,
Upon whose grassless floor of red-brown hue,
By sheddings from the pining umbrage tinged
Perenially—beneath whose sable roof
Of boughs, as if for festal purpose, decked
With unrejoicing berries—ghostly shapes
May meet at noon-tide ; Fear and trembling Hope,
Silence and Foresight ; Death the skeleton
And Time the shadow ;—there to celebrate,
As in a natural temple scattered o'er
With altars undisturbed of mossy stone,
United worship ; or in mute repose
To lie, and listen to the mountain flood
Murmuring from Glaramara's inmost caves."

The size attained by the yew in this district is astonishing. One, which for many years lay prostrate at the other end of Borrowdale, measured nine yards in circumference, and contained 1,460 cubic feet of wood. The famous Lorton Yew has about the same girth; appearing like a dark clump beside a white farmhouse.

In Patterdale churchyard there is another ancient and remarkably fine old yew tree, which attracts the notice of all visitors to that place, the trunk of which is to some extent decayed, being so split and divided that it presents several through openings. To this tree there is an excellent good story attached. Some years ago the then Bishop of London (Blomfield) and family were visiting the lakes, and in due course arrived at the "Sun" Hotel, Pooley Bridge, Ullswater. The boatman at the hotel, Tom Watt, an original, uneducated, but quick-witted individual, had the honour of rowing the party (there being no steamer on the lake at that time) up the lake from Pooley to Patterdale. On arriving at the latter place his lordship visited the "House of Prayer." In doing so he noticed the yew tree, and observing its shattered condition, exclaimed "that it must be very old." Tom, equal to the occasion, replied, and assured his lordship "that it was, being 9,999 years old." His lordship was astonished, and remarked "that it must have been there before the flood." Tom's ready rejoinder to this observation was, "Yes, doesn't your lordship see how the waters has washed holes through it." The Bishop was so pleased and amused with Tom's fertility of invention, that his guide received a reward, and the intimation "that it was the best story he had heard since leaving London."

DERWENTWATER.

Southey, writing to a friend, said :—"I have seen a sight more dreamy and wonderful than any scenery that fancy ever yet devised for fairy-land. We had walked down to the lake side; it was a delightful day, the sun shining, and a few white clouds hanging motionless in the sky. The opposite shore of Derwentwater consists of one long mountain, which suddenly terminates in an arch, and through that opening you see a long valley between mountains, and bounded by mountain beyond mountain; to the right of the arch the heights are more varied and of greater elevation. Now, as there was not a breath of air stirring, the surface of the lake was so perfectly still that it became one great mirror, and all its waters disappeared: the whole line of shore was represented as vividly and steadily as it existed in its being—the arch, the vale within, the single houses far within the vale, the smoke from their chimneys, the farthest hills, and the shades and substance joined at their bases so indivisibly, that you could make no separation even in your judgment. As I stood on the shore, heaven and the clouds seemed lying under me; I was looking down into the sky, and the whole range of mountains, having one line of summits under my feet, and another above me seemed to be suspended between the firmaments. Shut your eyes and dream of a scene so unnatural and so beautiful."

Southey declares in his "Colloquies" that the best general view of Derwentwater is from the terrace between Applethwaite and Millbeck, a little before the former hamlet. "The old roofs and chimneys of the hamlet," he continues, "come finely in the foreground, and the trees upon the Ormathwaite estate give there a richness to the middle ground which is wanting in other parts of the vale."

Miss Martineau says:—The islands of Derwentwater are full of historic interest. The Radcliffes possessed Lord's Island, the largest on the lake, which was once a part of the mainland, and traces of the family residence which stood there are still to be found. In the feudal times they cut a fosse, and set up a drawbridge. Everywhere there are traces of the unhappy family; even in the sky, the aurora borealis being sometimes called, to this day, Lord Derwentwater's lights, because it was particularly brilliant the night after his execution. Rampsholme, another of the islands, was theirs also, and the hermit, the dear friend of St. Cuthbert, who lived on St. Herbert's Isle in the seventh century, is somehow mixed up in legends, or local imaginations (which are careless of dates), with the same family. All that is known of St. Herbert is, that he really had a hermitage on the island, and that St. Cuthbert and he used to meet either at Lindisfarne or Derwentwater, once a year. The legend of their deaths is well known : namely, that, according to their prayer, they died on the same day. There is beauty in the tradition that the man of action and the man of meditation, the propagandist and the recluse, were so dear to each other, and so congenial. Vicar's or Derwent Isle, is the other of the four large islands, and a cool and fragrant bower it is. The Floating island,* whose appearance is announced at intervals of a few years, has obtained more celebrity than it deserves. It is a mass of soil and decayed vegetation, which rises when distended with gases, and sinks again when it has parted with them at the surface. Such is the explanation given by philosophers of this piece of natural magic, which has excited so much sensation during successive generations. Sometimes it comes up as a mere patch, and sometimes as large as an acre.

SOUTHER FELL.

ITS PHANTOM ARMY.—MIRAGE.

Souther Fell, a portion of the mountain Blencathra, or Saddleback, on the left of the road from Keswick

---

*There is no doubt that the rising of this so called Floating Island is caused by gas, evolved from decayed vegetable matter, by the action of the sun, as the Island rises only after a season of very hot weather.

to Penrith, is the very home of superstition and romance. This Souther, or Soutar Fell, is the mountain on which ghosts appeared in myriads at intervals during ten years of the last century, presenting the same appearance to twenty-six chosen witnesses, and to all the cottagers within view of the mountain, and for a space of two hours and a half at one time, the spectral show being closed by darkness! The mountain, be it remembered, is full of precipices, which defy all marching of bodies of men, and the north and west sides present a sheer perpendicular of 900 feet. On midsummer eve, 1735, a farm servant of a Mr. Lancaster, half a mile from the mountain, saw the eastern side of its summit covered with troops, who pursued their onward march for an hour. They came in distinct bodies from an eminence on the north end, and disappeared in a niche at the summit. When the poor fellow told his tale, he was insulted on all hands—as original observers usually are when they see anything wonderful. Two years after, also on a midsummer's eve, Mr. Lancaster saw some men there, apparently following their horses, as if they had returned from hunting. He thought nothing of this; but he happened to look up again ten minutes after, and saw the figures, now mounted and followed by an interminable array of troops, five abreast, marching from the eminence and over the cleft as before. All the family saw this, and the manœuvres of the force, as each company was kept in order by a mounted officer, who galloped this way and that. As the shades of twilight came on the discipline appeared to relax, and the troops intermingled and rode at unequal paces, till all was lost in darkness. Now, of course, all the Lancasters were insulted, as their servant had been: but their justification was not long delayed. On the midsummer eve of 1745, twenty-six persons, expressly summoned by the family, saw all that had been seen, and more. Carriages were now interspersed with the troops; and everybody knew that no carriages ever had been or could be on the summit of Souther Fell. The multitude was beyond imagination, for the troops filled a space of half a mile, and marched quickly, till night hid them—still marching. There was nothing vaporous or indistinct about the appearance of these spectres. So real did they seem, that some of the people went up next morning to look for the hoof-marks of the horses; and awful it was to them to find not one footprint on heather or grass. The witnesses attested the whole story on oath before a magistrate; and fearful were the expectations held by the whole country side about the coming events of the Scotch rebellion. It now came out that two others had seen something of the sort in the interval—viz., in 1743— but had concealed it, to escape the insults to which their neighbours were subjected. Mr. Wren, of Wilton Hall, and his farm-servant saw, one summer evening, a man and a dog on the mountain pursuing some horses along a place so steep that a horse could hardly by any possibility keep a footing on it. Their speed was prodigious, and their disappearance at the south end of the Fell so rapid, that Mr. Wren and the servant went up the next morning to find the body of the man, who must have been killed. Of the man, horse, or dog they found not a trace; and they came down and held their tongues. When they did speak, they fared not much better for having twenty-six sworn comrades in their disgrace. As for the explanation, the Editor of the *Lonsdale Magazine* declared (vol. ii., p. 313,) that it was discovered that on that midsummer eve of 1745, the rebels were "exercising on the western coast of Scotland, whose movements had been reflected by some transparent vapour, similar to the 'Fata Morgana' or the 'Spectre of the Brocken.'" This is not much in the way of explanation; but it is all that can be had. These facts, however, brought out many more: as the spectral march of the same kind seen in Leicestershire in 1707, and the tradition of the tramp of armies over Helvellyn on the eve of the battle of Marston Moor.

HELVELLYN.

That unfortunate " young lover of nature," Charles Gough, attempted to cross the mountain Helvellyn, by way of Striding Edge from Wythburn to Patterdale, one day in the early spring of 1805, after a fall of snow had partially concealed the path, and rendered it dangerous. It could never be ascertained whether he was killed by his fall, or perished with hunger. Let us hope that death came with friendly care to shorten sufferings that might have been yet more awful. Three months elapsed before the body was found, and then it was guarded by a faithful terrier bitch, his constant attendant during frequent solitary rambles through the wilds of Cumberland and Westmorland. The remains of the stranger now peacefully repose in the place of interment connected with the Friends' Meeting House at Tirril, near Penrith.

The following lines by Wordsworth, records this striking instance of brute fidelity :—

> " This dog had been through three months' space
> A dweller in that savage place ;
> Yes—proof was plain, that since the day
> On which the traveller thus had died,
> The dog had watched about the spot
> Or by his master's side.
> How nourished there through such a time,
> He knows, who gave that love sublime,
> And gave that strength of feeling great
> Above all human estimate."

Sir Walter Scott also immortalises this sad occurrence in his sonnet on " Helvellyn " :—

"I climb'd the dark brow of the mighty Helvellyn,
    Lakes and mountains beneath me gleam'd misty and wide ;
All was still, save by fits, when the eagle was yelling,
    And starting around me the echoes replied.
On the right, Striding Edge, round the Red Tarn was bending,
And Catchedicam its left verge was defending,
One huge nameless rock in the front was ascending,
    When I marked the sad spot where the wanderer had died.

" Dark green was that spot 'mid the brown mountain heather,
    Where the Pilgrim of Nature lay stretched in decay,
Like the corpse of an outcast abandoned to weather,
    Till the mountain winds wasted the tenantless clay.
Nor yet quite deserted, though lonely extended,
For, faithful in death, his mute favourite attended,
The much-loved remains of her master defended,
    And chased the hill-fox and the raven away.

" How long didst thou think that his silence was slumber?
    When the wind waved his garment, how oft didst thou start?
How many long days and long nights didst thou number,
    Ere he faded before thee, the friend of thy heart?
And, Oh! was it meet that—no requiem read o'er him,
No mother to weep and no friend to deplore him,
And thou, little guardian, alone stretched before him—
    Unhonour'd the Pilgrim from life should depart?

" When a prince to the fate of the peasant has yielded,
    The tapestry waves dark round the dim-lighted hall ;
With scutcheons of silver the coffin is shielded,
    And pages stand mute by the canopied pall :
Through the courts, at deep midnight, the torches are gleaming;
In the proudly-arched chapel the banners are beaming ;
Far adown the long aisle sacred music is streaming,
    Lamenting a chief of the people should fall.

" But meeter for thee, gentle lover of nature,
    To lay down thy head like the meek mountain lamb :
When, wilder'd, he drops from some cliff huge in stature,
    And draws his last sob by the side of his dam.
And more stately thy couch by this desert lake lying,
Thy obsequies sung by the grey plover flying,
With one faithful friend but to witness thy dying,
    In the arms of Helvellyn and Catchedicam."

DANGER OF ASCENDING MOUNTAINS IN WINTER.

A parallel case to that of Gough, occurred on the Great Gable, in the neighbourhood of Wastwater, in February, 1865. Mr. Lennox Butler was the son of the Hon. Mr. Butler, of Cottonhouse, Rugby, and about twenty-five years of age. He was a frequent visitor to the lake district in summer, and came at the close of January, 1865, to Keswick. He made the Derwentwater Hotel, Portinscale, his head quarters, which he left on the 2nd February, to explore, for a few days, Borrowdale and Wastdale Head. In the last-named place he remained at the house of Mr. Ritson, thence making frequent excursions. Among others, he ascended Scawfell, on which occasion he lost himself on his return, and had to remain with some shepherds all night.

On Wednesday, the 7th February, he went out at eleven o'clock in the morning, for the purpose of ascending the Great Gable, saying that he would be back in about three hours. Seeing nothing of him afterwards, Mr. Ritson concluded that he had gone to Keswick. Several days passed away, when Mr. Bell, the then landlord of the Derwentwater Hotel, becoming apprehensive that some accident had happened to Mr. Butler, wrote to Mr. Ritson on the subject of his non-appearance. Upon this, the latter started, with some other mountaineers, in search of their missing guest. They traced the marks of his snow shoes, to that part of the Great Gable Fell facing Wastwater and Ennerdale. On coming to a precipitous part they lost these tracks; but from the appearance of the snow, it seemed as if something had rolled down the mountain side.

As it was not safe to descend at this place, a retriever dog was sent down the steep, and when he had gone some 200 yards below, he halted and barked.

By a circuitous route the men gained the spot and there found the corpse of the hapless traveller covered with snow, only a portion of his plaid protruding. They carried him back to the house which he had left only a week before in robust health and excellent spirits. Upon examination, his skull was found to be dreadfully fractured, and a part of his upper lip gone. He had apparently lost his footing on the slippery platform of the mountain, and rolled down with terrific impetus, falling on his face. His hat and stick were found at some distance. The deceased gentleman was an enthusiastic admirer of English mountain scenery, and his face, as a visitor, was familiar in the neighbourhood of Keswick and the outlying districts, over which his awful death cast at the time a general gloom.

Since the above sad event another fatal occurrence took place, though the time was in the height of summer. A Mr. Barnard, of Angel Street, St. Martin's-le-Grand, London, started on a tour from Keswick, by way of Borrowdale, Sty-head Pass, Wastdale, Blacksail, through the head of the vale of Ennerdale, over Scarf Gap to Buttermere, and thence back to Keswick. He succeeded in his journey till he got into the vale of Ennerdale, where he, having apparently become fatigued by his difficult walk, sat down near a rock, and whether from heart disease or a chill, checking perspiration, and being without a companion, died. It was some weeks before his remains were found at some little distance away from the ordinary track. Many others have had narrow escapes; one of whom suggested that "The passes of Scarf Gap and Black Sail should not be attempted late in the season without a guide, for the following reasons:—A friend and myself left the inn at Buttermere on our way to Wastdale, in a heavy rain, being pressed for time. We reached the summit of Scarf Gap and descended into the Ennerdale Valley, with tolerable success, in spite of a cold north-east wind and driving rain; we also ascended Black Sail about half way, when my friend's pony, a hardy and powerful animal, came to a standstill. I then pushed on alone, on foot, to find a better track for the pony, and had attained so close to the summit as to see the platform, as it were, within my reach, when prolonged wet and cold produced such severe numbness and faintness, that I had barely strength to return to my companion, whom I found very little better off than myself. But for a flask of brandy in his bag, I do not think we could ever have left the valley alive; as it was, we had barely power to make our way through the swamps, rocks, and swollen torrents of the Liza. Never but once before did I feel so near the gates of death; and feel it a duty to save, so far as in me lies, my fellow creatures from so imminent a danger."

THE CATARACT OF LODORE.

[Written by the late Robert Southey, poet laureate, at Greta Hall, Keswick, for the amusement of his children.]

"How does the water
Come down at Lodore?"
My little boy ask'd me
Thus once on a time.
And moreover he task'd me
To tell him in rhyme,
Anon at the word.
Then first came one daughter
And then came another,
To second and third
The request of their brother,
And to hear how the water
Comes down at Lodore,
With its rush and its roar,
 As many a time
They had seen it before.
So I told them in rhyme,
For of rhymes I had store;

And 'twas in my vocation,
For their recreation,
That so I should sing;
Because I was laureate
To them and the King.

From its sources which well
In the tarn on the fell;
From its fountains
In the mountains
Its rills and its gills;
Through moss and through brake
It runs and it creeps
For awhile, till it sleeps
In its own little lake;
And thence at departing,
Awakening and starting,
It runs through the reeds
And away it proceeds,
Through meadow and glade,
In sun and in shade,
And through the wood shelter,
Among crags in its flurry,

    Helter—skelter,
    Hurry—skurry,

Here it comes sparkling,
And there it lies darkling;
Now smoking and frothing
Its tumult and wrath in
Till in this rapid race
On which it is bent,
It reaches the place
Of its steep descent.
The cataract strong
Then plunges along,
Striking and raging,
As if a war waging
Its caverns and rocks among;
Rising and leaping,
Sinking and creeping,
Swelling and sweeping,
Showering and springing,
Flying and flinging,
Writhing and ringing,
Eddying and whisking,
Turning and twisting,

Around and around,
With endless rebound!
Smiting and fighting,
A sight to delight in;
Confounding,
Astounding,
Dizzying and deafening the ear with its sound.

Collecting, projecting,
Receding and speeding,
And shocking and rocking,
And darting and parting,
And threading and spreading,
And whizzing and hissing,
And dripping and skipping,
And hitting and spitting,
And shining and twining
And rattling and battling.
And shaking and quaking,
And pouring and roaring,
And waving and raving,
And tossing and crossing,
And flowing and going,
And running and stunning,
And foaming and roaming,
And dinning and spinning,
And dropping and hopping,
And working and jerking,
And juggling and struggling,
And heaving and cleaving,
And moaning and groaning,
And glittering and frittering,
And gathering and feathering,
And whitening and brightening,
And quivering and shivering,
And hurrying and skurrying,
And thundering and floundering.

Dividing, and gliding, and sliding,
And falling, and brawling, and sprawling,
And driving, and riving, and striving,
And sprinkling, and twinkling, and wrinkling,
And sounding and bounding, and rounding,
And bubbling and troubling and doubling,
And grumbling, and rumbling, and tumbling,
And clattering, and battering, and shattering,

Retreating, and beating, and meeting, and sheeting,
Delaying, and straying and playing, and spraying,

Advancing, and prancing, and glancing, and dancing,
Recoiling turmoiling, and toiling, and boiling,
And gleaming and streaming, and steaming and beaming,
And rushing, and flushing, and brushing, and gushing,
And flapping, and rapping, and clapping, and slapping,
And curling, and whirling, and purling, and twirling,
And thumping, and plumping, and bumping, and jumping,
And dashing, and flashing, and splashing, and clashing,
And so never ending, but always descending,
Sounds and motions for ever and ever are blending,
All at once, and all o'er, with a mighty uproar,
And this way the water comes down at Lodore.

DUNMAIL RAISE.

'Twixt Cumberland and Westmorland
   There stands a pile of stones;
'Tis said to mark the resting place
   Of "brave King Dunmail's bones."

Seat Sandal on the east looks down,
   And on the west Steel Fell;
And could their hoary summits speak,
   The history they might tell:

How Scotch and Saxon monarchs,
   Nine hundred years ago,
Had joined their arms against Dunmail
   To strike a crushing blow.

And here he met the forces twain,
   And made a gallant stand
For hearth, and home, and liberty,
   And his native Cumberland.

But here he fell, and many more
   Brave warriors of the west;
And this, the cairn, his followers built
   To show his place of rest.

In Grisedale Tarn his crown was sunk—
   For ever lost to view;
But this, his rugged monument,
   Has stood long ages through.

But dalesmen give another name—
  A different story tell ;
And by "The Devil's Stoneheap"
  The pile is known right well.

They say that long, long years ago,
  The hero of the tale
Took up an apronful of stones
  To bear across the vale.

With careful steps he downward came
  So far, and all went well ;
When lo ! the apron-string gave way
  And down the boulders fell.

And to this day they're lying there—
  'Tis said they always will—
And many a traveller knows it
  As " The Devil's Stoneheap " still.

A MIRAGE ON SKIDDAW.

The following account of a very remarkable mirage was written by a " Cumbrian " to the publisher. He had, at the time, resided in the modern Babylon about sixty years, and who, being deeply absorbed in business there, had probably never heard or read of the " Spectre of the Brocken," or the " Spectre Army of Souther Fell," as will be seen from his statement. On the occasion of one of his visits to his native place, he, in company with two friends, ascended Skiddaw, for the purpose of viewing a " rolling sea of mountains," they became, unexpectedly, spectators of, in this locality, a rare phenomena—a mirage. He said :— "Although I have now (1854) resided fifty-four years in and near the metropolis, I have, in every three or four years of that time, visited my native hills of Cumberland, which I left at twenty years of age. The ' everlasting hills' remain, and Skiddaw, to my eye, increases each time in lofty majesty ! but my early friends once surrounding its base, Where are they ? I might repeat

(I think with Byron), "Echo says, Where are they?" My affection for the grand and romantic scenery remains as strong as ever, but many of my visits have been clouded by the remembrance of dear departed friends.

It is curious to reflect how little the inhabitants of England generally know of their own country; but now that facilities are so great, it must surely become otherwise—now that a summer's day can, at a trifling expense and no trouble, set the London passenger down at the beautiful lake of Windermere,* and a beautiful morning's ride then places him at the foot of Skiddaw, after passing through Bowness, Ambleside, and by Rydal Mount (which must be endeared to many as the abode of our departed Wordsworth, and still the residence of his aged and amiable widow, with both of whom I had the happiness to be acquainted); then by the lakes of Rydal, Grasmere, &c., until coming to the top of the hill overlooking the Vale of Keswick, the eye revels with delight unutterable over the lakes of Derwentwater and Bassenthwaite, and the indescribable scenery surrounding them. With such an evening sky as Wordsworth knew well how to choose, I would venture to say with him, 'That in many points of view our lakes are much more interesting than those of the Alps.'

When I took up my pen it was to tell an unvarnished tale, 'not at the expense of truth,' for the circumstance was witnessed by myself. Such an appearance I never heard recorded of the Alps, the Hartz mountains, or any other mountains of the globe; and thus I claim for Skiddaw a pre-eminence which I wish my own countrymen to appreciate. This adventure I have often told to my friends (some of whom may possibly

---

* The railway from Penrith to Keswick and Cockermouth was not then constructed.

read this), but I have never before given it to the public. Now to my tale :

On the 4th of October, 1820, I, with two friends (one of whom, a relative, is now no more), set out from Cockermouth at seven in the morning, and walked to Bassenthwaite, about seven miles. We ascended Skiddaw on that side, which is more steep than the ascent from Keswick, being about three and the other five miles to the summit. The morning was beautifully fine until we had completed about one-third of our way up, when we were suddenly surprised by rain, and we could no longer see the fine prospect around us. We had no guide, and had got upon some swampy ground, which made me consider it unsafe to go on, and I proposed to return. My friends, however, were more courageous, and we had not proceeded more than a quarter of an hour before we saw the rainy cloud which had immersed us pass away at our feet, and over it the whole country beaming in the sunshine. We now 'went on our way rejoicing,' stopping occasionally to rest and to enjoy the constantly expanding view. The sky was serene when we arrived at the top, and not a cloud visible, save a few fleecy ones rolling slowly along the side of the mountain, considerably below us. The air seemed more agreeable than that of a summer's day: exercise had, no doubt, contributed to the warmth and comfort which we felt. To attempt a description of the scenery here would be vain. I advise every lover of nature to go and see it.

I have already been too prolix, but now comes the pith of my story. We had to call on my friend, Mr. Slack (now no more), who then lived at Red House, on the south-western side of the mountain, and, to do this, go down by what is called Ullock Pyke, a narrow ridge, on the right of which, as you descend, is a terrific chasm, on whose border we had to walk on a line with each other; and I think at the time we were about six yards apart. On the left we had a declivity of greensward ; we were obliged to step carefully for our own safety, and could not, therefore, now look around us. Suddenly we perceived this great cavity to be fearfully gloomy, as if filled with a dense fog, or by something we did not comprehend, and the dark gigantic figure of a man, as standing on a cloud, right before us in the centre of a luminous ring of about twelve feet diameter, of the most vivid prismatic colours of the rainbow, and at the apparent distance of about ten yards, the circle extending about two feet above the head and the like beneath the feet. For the moment we were awe-stricken. My yet surviving friend exclaimed, ' Tremendous! just like Jesus Christ!' There was now a silent pause, but in a minute we looked calmly on the figure before us, and still considered it independent of ourselves—that is, that we had nothing to do with its formation. It was then two o'clock. The sun shone brightly upon where we stood, and his rays passed us into the dark abyss, at the oblique angle consequent on the time of the year and on the time of the day. One of us accidentally made some gesticulation, and saw that the figure did likewise, and then called out, ' It's my figure!' Another, holding up his hand, said 'No, it's mine!' and so said the third. Thus we found that, although one figure only was visible to all of us, yet *that* was a magnified one of himself, and that the beautiful circular iris was reflected to his own eye alone, and, had there been twenty of us, each and all would have seen but one appearance. The whole, I think, lasted not more than five or six minutes, when the vivid colours gradually faded, the opaque figure began to be transparent, and the gulf again clear as the scenery around us.

My idea is that this effect might possibly be the result of a fleecy cloud, such as we had frequently seen that day rolling up the chasm, of a sufficient density to refract the sun's rays and operate as a concave mirror to give back the human forms magnified to about eight feet in height; but this is a crude suggestion only. I do not wonder that the simple peasantry of mountainous countries are often superstitious.

So many circumstances must combine to produce what I have endeavoured to describe, that I fear visitors may often traverse Ullock Pyke and never see the like again.

We then descended quickly by the enclosure of firs to Mr. Slack's house, and having told what we thought our wondrous tale, and eaten with great zest some cold refreshment, accompanied with tea, we walked back to Cockermouth, reverently impressed by the sermons which mountains and lakes so eloquently preach, and without being too fatigued to have a sound sleep at night.
J. B.

KESWICK OR DERWENTWATER REGATTA IN THE OLDEN TIME.

A regatta, which took place on the 6th of September, 1782, is thus described: At eight o'clock in the morning a vast concourse of ladies and gentlemen appeared on the side of the Derwent Lake, where a number of marquees, extending about 400 yards, were erected for their accommodation. At twelve, such of the company as were invited by Mr. Pocklington, passed over in boats to the island which bears his name (now known as Derwent Isle); and, on their landing, were saluted by a discharge of his artillery. This might properly be called the opening of the regatta; for as soon as the echo of this discharge had ceased, a signal gun was fired, and five boats, which lay upon their oars (on that part of the water which runs nearest the town of Keswick), instantly pushed off the shore, and began the race.

A view from any of the attendants' boats (of which there were several) presented a scene which beggars all description. The sides of the hoary mountains were clad with spectators, and the glassy surface of the lake was variegated with a number of pleasure barges, which, tricked out in all the gayest colours, and glittering in the rays of a meridian sun, gave a new appearance to the celebrated beauties of this matchless vale.

The contending boats passed Pocklington's Island, and, rounding St. Herbert's and Rampsholm, edged down by the outside of Lord's Island, describing in the race almost a perfect circle, and during the greatest part, in full view of the company.

About three o'clock, preparations were made for the sham attack on Pocklington's Island. The fleet (consisting of several barges, armed with small cannon and muskets) retired out of view, behind Friars Crag, to prepare for action; previous to which, a flag of truce was sent to the Governor, with a summons to surrender upon honourable terms. A defiance was returned; soon after which the fleet was seen advancing, with great spirit, before the batteries, and instantly forming into a curved line, a terrible cannonade began on both sides, accompanied with a dreadful discharge of musketry. This continued for some time, and being echoed from hill to hill, in an amazing variety of sounds, filled the ear with whatever could produce astonishment and awe. All nature seemed to be in an uproar, which impressed on the awakened imagination the most lively ideas of the 'war of elements' and crush of worlds.

After a severe conflict, the enemies were driven from the attack, in great disorder. A *feu de joie* was then fired in the fort, and oft repeated by the responsive echoes. The fleet, after a little delay, formed again, and practising a great variety of beautiful manœuvres, renewed the attack. Uproar again sprang up, and the deep-toned echoes of the mountains again joined in the solemn chorus, which was heard to the distance of ten leagues to leeward, through the eastern opening of that vast amphitheatre, as far as Appleby.

The garrison at length capitulated, and the entertainments of the water being finished (towards evening) the company moved to Keswick; to which other place from the water's edge, a range of lamps was fixed, very happily disposed, and a number of fireworks were played off.

An assembly-room (which had been built for the purpose) next received the ladies and gentlemen, and a dance concluded this annual festivity; a chain of amusements which, we may venture to assert, no other town can possibly furnish, and which wants only to be more universally known to render it a place of more general resort than any other in the kingdom.

To those whom nature's works alone can charm, this spot will, at all times, be viewed with rapture and astonishment; but no breast, however unsusceptible of pleasure, can be indifferent to that display o every beauty which decks the ancient vale of Keswick on a *regatta day.*

ST. HERBERT AND HIS ISLE.

St. Herbert's Island, about four acres in extent, is densely covered with trees; its situation is very central in the lake, and contained a curious octagonal grotto or cottage, built with unhewn stones, mossed over, and thatched; its site is near that of an ancient hut said to have been occupied by St. Herbert, the ruins of which are left untouched. Respecting this recluse it is related that St. Herbert, a priest and confessor, who, to avoid the intercourse of man, and that nothing might withdraw his attention from unceasing mortification and prayer, chose this island for his abode. The scene around him was well adapted to the severity of his religious life. He was surrounded with the lakes, from whence he received his diet. On every hand, the voice of waterfalls excited the most solemn strains of meditation—rocks and mountains were his daily prospect, inspiring his mind with ideas of the might and majesty of his Creator; and were suitable to his disposition of soul. Silence seemed to take up her eternal abode. From the situation of this island, nature hath given one half of the year to impetuous hurricanes and storms. Here this recluse erected an hermitage, the remains of which appear to this day, being built of stone and mortar, formed into two apartments. The outer one, about twenty feet by sixteen, has probably been his chapel; the other of narrower dimensions, his cell, and apparently a little garden adjoining.

Bede, in his history of the Church of England, writes thus of this saint:—There was a certain priest, revered for his uprightness and perfect life and manners, named Herbert, who had a long time been in union with the man of God (St. Cuthbert of Farne Isle) in the bond of spiritual love and friendship; for living a solitary life in the isle of that great and extended lake from whence proceeds the river of Derwent, he used to visit St. Cuthbert every year, to receive from his lips the doctrine of eternal life. When this holy priest heard of St. Cuthbert coming to Luguballia, he came after his usual manner, desiring to be comforted more and more with the hopes of everlasting bliss by his divine exhortations. As they sat together, the Bishop said, "Remember, brother Hereberte, that whatsoever ye have to say and ask of me, you do it now, for after we depart hence, we shall not meet again, and see one another corporally in this world; for I know well the time of my dissolution is at hand, and the laying aside of this earthly tabernacle draweth on apace!" When Hereberte heard this, he fell down at his feet, and with many sighs and tears, "beseeched him, for the love of the Lord, that he would not forsake him, but to remember his faithful brother and associate, and make intercession with the gracious God, that they might depart hence into heaven together, to behold his grace and glory whom they had in unity of spirit served on earth; for you know I have ever studied and laboured for him according to your pious and virtuous instructions; and in whatsoever I offended or omitted through ignorance and frailty I straightway used my earnest efforts to amend after your ghostly counsel, will, and judgment!" At this earnest and affectionate request of Hereberte's, the Bishop went to prayer, and presently being certified in spirit that his petition to heaven would be granted. "Arise," said he, "my dear brother; weep not, but let your rejoicing be with exceeding gladness, for the great mercy of God hath granted unto us our prayer." The truth of which promise and prophecy was well proved in that which ensued; for their separation was the last that befel them on earth: on the same day, which was the 19th day of March, their souls departed from their bodies, and were straight in union in the beatific sight and vision; and were transported hence to the kingdom of heaven by the service and hand of angels.

It is probable the hermit's little oratory or chapel might be kept in repair after his death, as a particular veneration appears to have been paid by the religious of after ages to this retreat, and the memory of the saints. There is a variance in the accounts given by authors of the day of the saints' deaths: Bede says the 19th day of March; other authors on the 20th day of May, A.D. 687; and by a record given in Bishop Appleby's Register, it would appear that the 13th day of April was observed as the solemn anniversary. But, however, in the year 1734, at the distance of almost seven centuries, we find this place resorted to in holy services and processions, and the hermit's memory celebrated in religious offices.

THE WONDERS OF SADDLEBACK.

The following description of the incidents experienced by a party of visitors to Saddleback (a very rare occurrence), we give in the words of one of the number, and will be found very interesting :—

"When we had ascended about a mile up that portion known as Scales Fell, one of the party, on looking round, was so astonished with the different appearance of objects in the valley, so far beneath us, that he declined proceeding. We had not gone much further, till the other companion (of the relator) was suddenly taken ill, and wished to return. I was almost ready to give up my project, which I should have done with great reluctance, as the day was remarkably favourable, and exhibited every scene to the greatest advantage. We were assured that if we proceeded a little way, we should find a resting-place, where the second defaulter might recover from the effects of his journey. After labouring another half-hour, we gained the margin of an immense cavity, in the side of the mountain, the bottom of which formed a wide basin, and was filled with water; that from our station looked black, though smooth as glass, covering the space of from 25 to 35 acres. It is said to be so deep that the sun never shines upon it, and that the reflection of the stars may be seen therein at noon-day; but that was a curiosity we did not enjoy. From our station there was a gentle declivity to a smooth and verdant lawn, several yards in breadth, which was the situation our guide had promised us; and the descent thereto led us about half-way to the lake: a like easy descent would have led us to the edge of the lake, round which there was a broad green walk; but our leader informing us of the danger of passing that slippery path, we did not proceed. We now contemplated the scene with *awe-struck wonder*. We stood directly facing the middle of the mountain, the form of which gives it the name of *Saddleback*: and to the lake a perpendicular rocky precipice presented itself, extending to the north-east side of the mountain called Foul-crag. To the right hand, the steepness of the rocks gradually declined; above us, and on the left, they were stupendous and perpendicular; so that in one half of the circle the rocks were lofty and precipitous, whilst in the other half they gradually decreased. My fellow-traveller would proceed no further; and, with my guide, I was left to explore the other parts of the mountain. Winding round, and keeping the cavity on our right, we attained the ridge or summit of the rock, where we found a passage three or four yards broad: on the right, the descent to the lake looked truly awful; whilst the steep rocks on the other side were lofty, and not to be climbed by human steps. This passage, some hundred yards in length, may be compared to a bridge covered with grass. Having reached the summit, we went to the point nearest to Keswick vale, and there enjoyed a most delightful prospect; from thence we passed to the next point, being Foul-crag, with Skiddaw on the left; from whence we looked down into a dreadful abyss, the bottom of which the eye could not penetrate: sheep frequently perish in this place, as the number of dead carcasses and skeletons evinced. We walked back by the side next to the lake; but to look down from thence was so terrible, I could not endure it a moment. We perceived from thence, that my companion, whom we had last left, was laid upon the ground; I pressed the guide to hasten to him, but he refused, alleging that a fog was rising, and it would be very hazardous for me to explore my way alone down the mountain. In a short time we were enveloped in a very dense vapour, so that we were obliged to keep near to each other; the sudden change was almost incredible. It was with difficulty my guide regained the passage, or dry bridge, which we missed on several attempts; and one incautious step would have plunged us in the horrid abyss. The fog soon afterwards dispersed, as precipitately as it came on, and left us again under a serene sky. We passed to the foot of Foul-crag, to view its wonderful precipices from their base; and again safely reached our destination, after a laborious travel of four hours.

On the side of the mountain we found several large plots of the *Lycopodium Clavatum*, or Club Moss; the creeping branches of which were closely matted and interwoven, and formed a carpet that seemed to surpass the workmanship of the finest artists.

THE BOWDER STONE, BORROWDALE.

The Boulder or Bowder Stone is an immense block of rock, and is supposed at some time to have become detached and fallen from the mountain side above. It rests on so small a base as to allow persons on its opposite sides to shake hands through a hole under it near the ground. Its length is 62 feet, height 36 feet, circumference 89 feet, and is computed to weigh 1,971 tons, and is supposed to be the largest separate piece of rock in the world. The following lines in the third book of Wordsworth's " Excursion " is very *apropos* to this mass of granite :—

> "Upon a semicirque of turf-clad ground,
> The hidden nook discovered to our view,
> A mass of rock, resembling, as it lay
> Right at the foot of that moist precipice,
> A stranded ship, with keel upturned, that rests
> Fearless of winds and waves."

DRUID'S CIRCLE, KESWICK.

The circle is formed of 38 stones, the largest of which is upwards of seven feet high and several tons in weight; and on the eastern side, within the circle, there are ten other stones. This monument of an unknown past is in a good state of preservation. If, as is popularly believed, it was a Druidical temple, its commanding position must have served to impress a feeling of solemnity on the devotees. What means the Druids had of bringing and placing these stones in their present position is a mystery of which there is not the faintest trace; their appliances must have been very powerful, more so than the present generation is disposed to give them credit for. Again, it is equally a mystery as to where they procured the stones—they must have been brought from a considerable distance, probably from the river Greta below; and then comes the question, How were they got up the hill to their respective positions? As Southey observed, "the spot is the most commanding that could be chosen, short of a mountain side;" and it is indeed nearly surrounded by mountains.

The old legend about the last human sacrifice of the Druids may belong to any of the monuments of that age in the district, and is probably claimed for them all. According to that old story: When some people settled in a clearing of the woods, beside a river, somewhere to the south of the district, the priests took up their station further north, among the mountains, where there were plenty of stones, fit and ready for their temple. After a time a fever laid waste the lower settlement, and the oracle demanded a sacrifice to appease the divine wrath. The lot fell on a young girl who was betrothed; and, on an appointed day, she was conveyed, with all the ceremonies, to the temple. A small hut of wickerwork, like a large bee-hive, was found set up on the western side of the temple. The girl was led into the circle and placed in the midst, while the dedication proceeded. We are even told that she was adorned with an oak garland, and held mistletoe in her hand. The whole population was looking on from a distance, but it must have been within reasonable reach, as everyone was required to contribute a stick to the fire. The wretched lover saw all from afar, and he daringly resolved—let the god be as wrathful as he pleased—not to contribute so much as a twig to the burning of his beloved. She was seen to enter the door, which was next to the circle, and then the priest closed it up, and heaped dry leaves and sticks that were brought all round the hut. The Arch-Druid in the meantime was procuring fire from two pieces of wood. He succeeded, and set the pile in a blaze. In this moment of despetration the lover saw every mountain round give foreh a great cataract, and all the floods gushed to the tlmple as to a centre, and made an island of the litt.e hut, returning when they had extinguished the fire The victim came forth with not a hair singed, and not a leaf of her garland withered. The Arch-Druid, skilled to interpret thunder, seems to have understood in this case the voice of the waters; for he announced that, henceforth, the god would have no more sacrifices.

Any visitor who may be sufficiently familiar with the residents, and can get them to speak their minds fully, will probably find that they still hold to the notion that no person can count the Druid stones correctly. There are in such circles smaller stones cropping out of the ground, which some visitors will, and others will not, include among those of the circle.

WHAT IS A MOUNTAIN?

A correspondent of *Notes and Queries* writes:—I have been led to make this query by a remark in an article in the *Times*, June, 1880. In speaking of the geographical features of England, the writer says, "We have no mountains." As I have, during the last few weeks, ascended the *mountains* Scawfell Pike, Helvellyn, and Skiddaw, this remark of the *Times* made me feel rather small. When I had accomplished Scawfell Pike, which is 3,200 feet high, and inaccessible even by mountain ponies for the last mile or so, I certainly felt, like Master Silence, that I had "done somewhat," and yet, when I returned home, I am told, on the high authority of the *Times*, that there are no mountains in England. The three mountains above mentioned are all over 3,000 feet in height. If this does not entitle an elevation to be called a mountain, what height does entitle it to be so called? It is no doubt true enough that 3,000 feet is a very small affair compared with the 15,000 feet of Mont Blanc or Monte Rosa, but then so is 4,400, the height of Ben Nevis. The last named, the highest mountain in Scotland, is about 1,200 feet higher than Scawfell Pike, the highest in England; but this, when compared with the prodigious heights of the Himalayas or the Andes, is not worth mentioning. It would accordingly be equally true to say there are no mountains in Scotland, which seems like a *reductio ad absurdum*. Lovers of Wordsworth cannot but feel thankful that the poet's lot was not cast in the present time. I feel that the destruction of the beautiful lake of Thirlmere, or, at any rate, its conversion into a great tank, which is much the same thing, would have been a life-long sorrow to him. If, in addition to this, he had been told on the authority of the chief organ in Europe, that it was nothing but a delusion to suppose that his beloved Helvellyn and Skiddaw are really mountains, he would have felt that insult was added to injury indeed.

ABBOTS OF FURNESS.

When the Abbots of Furness owned the whole of Borrowdale, a few monks were placed at its entrance to receive and guard the crops, and the hamlet of Grange was their granary.

THE BORROWDALE CUCKOO.

A gentleman now deceased (known to the writer) who was a resident and owner of property in the far-famed vale of Borrowdale—one of a jocular disposition, though still a *gentleman*, used to enjoy amazingly, when on his way home on horseback from Keswick, the fun of the boys who ran after him and shouted "cuckoo." If they performed their part well they, were sure to be rewarded with coins of the realm for their attentions to him. Of Borrowdale many curious tales are told, and which are enjoyed and laughed at by the inhabitants as excellent stories to amuse the public. One story is that a party of these dalesmen were once escorting a waggon-load of their valuable black-lead to London, and it being the days when thieves and highwaymen abounded, they were all armed with blunderbusses to guard their treasure. Resting the first night at Keswick, they were sheltered in one of the inns there, the waggon being placed in the entrance gateway, which was closed by large doors, the men taking it in turns to watch. Now it so happened that the owner of the house possessed, what was then rather uncommon, a cuckoo clock; when the hour of ten came round the clock began to strike, saying in slow and measured time, "Cuckoo." The Borrowdalians, thinking some of the town-folk, hearing of their arrival, had come to mock, threatened, if the words were repeated, to fire be the consequences what they might. The clock, of course, was deaf to the threats of the enraged and mortified man, and went on repeating "Cuckoo." This was too much for him—the Borrowdalian—so he fired upon his supposed jesters.

Tradition has it that upon one occasion the Borrowdalians decided, as spring time was so very charming, to enjoy a perennial one; and the sound of the cuckoo being so gladsome in the vale, to build a wall to keep in the cuckoo, and so have it for ever. They, it is alleged, built a wall across the entrance at Grange. The plan did not answer, but that was because, according to popular belief, from generation to generation, the wall was not built one course higher. It was simply on account of the wall being just too low that the cuckoo flew over, and so eternal spring does not reign in Borrowdale.

It is also said that an old Borrowdale man, in days past, went forth with horse and sacks (for there were no carts, because there was no roads) to bring home lime from beyond Keswick. On his return, when he was near Grange, it began to rain, and the man was alarmed at seeing his sacks begin to smoke. He got a handful of water from the river, but the smoke grew worse. Assured at length that the devil must be where there was any fire which was aggravated by water, he tossed the whole load over into the river.

Another anecdote shows, however, that a bright genius occasionally appeared among them. A "'statesman" (an "estatesman," or small proprietor) went one day to a distant fair, or sale, and brought home what neither he nor his neighbours had ever seen before—a pair of stirrups. Home he came jogging with his feet in his stirrups, but, by the time he had reached his own door, he had jammed his feet in so fast that they would not come out. There was great alarm and lamentation; but as it could not be helped now, the good man sat on his horse in the pasture for a day or two, his family bringing him food, till the eldest son, vexed to see the horse suffering by exposure, proposed to bring them both into the stable. This was done; and there sat the farmer for several days, his food being brought to him as before. At length it struck the second son that it was a pity not to make his father useful and release the horse; so he proposed to carry him, on the saddle, into the house. By immense exertion it was done; the horse being taken alongside the midden in the yard to ease the fall, and the good man found himself under his own roof again, spinning wool in a corner of the kitchen. There the mounted man sat spinning, through the cleverness of his second son, till the lucky hour arrived of the return of the youngest son, who was a scholar—a learned student from St. Bees. After duly considering the case he gave his counsel. He suggested that his father should draw his feet out of his shoes. This was done, amid the blessings of the family, and the good man was restored to his occupation and to liberty. The wife was so delighted that she said if she had a score of children, and had to begin life again she would make them all scholars.

Another native genius on one occasion came to a conclusion so striking that it is doubtful whether any University could rival it. A stranger came riding into the dale on a mule, and being bound for the mountains, went up the pass on foot, leaving the animal in the care of the host. The host had never seen such a creature before, nor had his neighbours. Fearing mischief, they consulted the wise man of the dale, for they kept a Sagum, or medicine man, to supply their deficiencies. He came, and after an examination of the mule, drew a circle round it, and consulted his books, while his charms were burning, and at length announced that he had found it out; the creature must be, he concluded, a peacock. So Borrowdale could then boast, without a rival, of a visit from a stranger who came riding on a peacock.

HAMLET OF STAIR.

The employment of the inhabitants of Stair, about 2½ miles from Keswick, at one time were fully occupied in woollen manufacture—an ancient staple of the district, as is shown by the inscription which has come down from the olden time, engraved on a flagstone :—

> "May God Almighty grant His aid
> To Keswick and its woollen trade."

Near the mill is a farm-house, said to have been built by the celebrated General Fairfax, whose initials are cut on the stone over the entrance door.

DESCRIPTION OF THE SCENERY IN A RIDE OVER SKIDDAW IN 1794.

Having engaged a guide, and with horses accustomed to the labour, we began to ascend this tremendous mountain by a way which makes the summit six miles from Keswick. Passing through bowery lanes, luxuriant with mountain ash, holly, and a variety of beautiful shrubs, to a broad, open common, a road led us the foot of Latrigg, or, as it is called by the country to people, Skiddaw's Cub, a large round hill, covered with heath, turf, and browsing sheep. A narrow path now wound along steep green precipices, the beauty of which prevented what danger there was from being perceived. Derwentwater was concealed by others that rose above them, but that part of the vale of Keswick which separates the two lakes and spreads a rich level of three miles was immediately below, Crosthwaite Church nearly in the centre, with the vicarage rising among the trees. More under shelter of Skiddaw, where the vale spreads into a sweet retired nook, lay the house and grounds of Ormathwaite.

Beyond the level opened a glimpse of Bassenthwaite-water, a lake which may be called elegant, bounded on one side by well-wooded rocks, and on the other by Skiddaw.

Soon after we rose above the steeps which had concealed Derwentwater, and it appeared with all its enamelled banks, sunk deep amidst a chaos of mountains, and surrounded by ranges of fells not visible from below. On the other hand, the more cheerful lake of Bassenthwaite expanded at its entire length. Having gazed awhile on this magnificent scene, we pursued the path, and soon after reached the brink of a chasm, on the opposite side of which wound our future track, for the ascent is here in an acutely zigzag direction. The horses carefully picked their steps along the narrow precipice, and turned the angle that led them to the opposite side.

At length, as we ascended, Derwentwater dwindled on the eye to the smallness of a pond, while the grandeur of its amphitheatre was increased by new ranges of dark mountains, no longer individually great, but so from accumulation; a scenery to give ideas of the breaking up of a world. Other precipices soon hid it again, but Bassenthwaite continued to spread immediately below us, till we turned into the heart of Skiddaw, and were enclosed by its steeps. We had now lost all tracks, even of the flocks that were scattered over these tremendous wilds. The guide conducted us by many curvings among the heathy hills and hollows of the mountain; but the ascents were such that the horses panted in the slowest walk, and it was necessary to let them rest every six or seven minutes. An opening to the south at length showed the whole plan of the narrow vales of St. John and Naddale, separated by the dark ridge of rock, called St. John's Rigg, with each its small line of verdure at the bottom, and bounded by enormous grey fells, which we were, however, now high enough to overlook.

A white speck on the top of St. John's Rigg was

pointed out by the guide to be a chapel of ease to Crosthwaite Church, Keswick, which has no less than five such scattered among the fells. From this chapel, dedicated to St. John, the rock and the vale have received their name, and our guide told us that Naddale was frequently known by the same title.

Leaving this view, the mountain soon again shut out all prospect, but of its own valleys and precipices, covered with various shades of turf and moss, and with heath, of which a dark purple was the prevailing hue. Not a tree or bush appeared on Skiddaw, nor even a stone wall anywhere broke the simple greatness of its lines. Sometimes we looked into tremendous chasms where the torrent, heard roaring long before it was seen, had worked itself a channel, and fell from ledge to ledge, foaming and shining amidst the dark rock. These streams are sublime from the length and precipitancy of their course, which, hurrying the sight with them into the abyss, act, as it were, in sympathy upon the nerves, and to save ourselves from following we recoil from the view with involuntary horror. Of such, however, we saw only two, and those by some departure from the usual course up the mountain; but everywhere met gushing springs, till we were within two miles of the summit, when our guide added to the rum in his bottle what he said was the last water we should find in our ascent.

The air now became very thin, and the steeps still more difficult of ascent; but it was often delightful to look down into the green hollows of the mountains, among pastoral scenes, that wanted only some mixture of wood to render them enchanting.

About a mile from the summit the way was, indeed, dreadfully sublime, lying, for nearly half-a-mile, along the ledge of a precipice, that passed with a swift descent for probably near a mile into a glen within the heart of Skiddaw; and not a bush or a hillock interrupted its vast length, or, by offering a mid-way check in the descent, diminished the fear it inspired. The ridgy steeps of Saddleback formed the opposite boundary of the glen, and, though really at a considerable distance, had, from the height of the two mountains, such an appearance of nearness that it almost seemed as if we could spring to its side. How much, too, did simplicity increase the sublime of this scenery, in which nothing but mountain, heath, and sky appeared.

But our situation was too critical or too unusual to permit the just impressions of such sublimity. The hill rose so closely above the precipice as scarcely to allow a ledge wide enough for a single horse. We followed the guide in silence, and, till we gained the more open wild, had no leisure for exclamation. After this the ascent appeared easy and secure, and we were bold enough to wonder that the steeps near the beginning of the mountains had excited any anxiety.

At length, passing the skirts of the two points of Skiddaw which are nearest to Derwentwater, we approached the third and loftiest, and then perceived that their steep sides, together with the ridges which connected them, were entirely covered near the summits with a whitish shivered slate, which threatens to slide down them with every gust of wind. The broken state of this slate makes the present summits seem like the ruins of others; a circumstance as extraordinary in appearance as difficult to be accounted for.

The ridge on which we passed from the neighbourhood of the second summit to the third was narrow, and the eyes reached, on each side, down the whole extent of the mountain, following, on the left, the rocky precipices that impend over the lake of Bassenthwaite, and looking, on the right, into the glens of Saddleback, far, far below. But the prospects that burst upon us from every part of the vast horizon, when we had gained the summit, were such as we had scarcely dared to hope for, and must now rather venture to enumerate than to describe.

We stood on a pinnacle commanding the whole dome of the sky. The prospects below, each of which had been before considered separately as a great scene, were now miniature parts of the immense landscape. To the north lay, like a map, the vast tract of low country which extends between Bassenthwaite and the Irish Channel, marked with the silver circles of the river Derwent, in its progress from the lake. Workington and its white coast were distinctly seen, and Cockermouth seemed almost under the eye. A long blackish line, more to the west, resembling a faintly-formed cloud, was said by the guide to be the Isle of Man, who, however, had the honesty to confess that the mountains of Down, in Ireland, which have been sometimes thought visible, had never been seen by him in the clearest weather.

Bounding the low country to the north, the wide Solway Frith, with its indented shores, looked like a grey horizon, and the double range of Scottish mountains, seen dimly through the mist beyond, like lines of dark clouds above it. The Solway appeared surprisingly near us, though at twenty miles distance, and the guide said that on a bright day its shipping could be plainly discerned.

Nearly in the north the heights seemed to soften into plains, for no object was there visible through the obscurity that had begun to draw over the further distance; but, towards the east, they appeared to swell again, and what we were told were the Cheviot hills dawned feebly beyond Northumberland. We now spanned the narrowest part of England, looking from the Irish Channel on the one side to the German Ocean on the other, which latter was, however, so far off as to be discernible like mist.

Nearer than the county of Durham stretched the ridge of Crossfell, and an indistinct multitude of the Westmorland and Yorkshire highlands, whose lines disappear behind Saddleback, now evidently preeminent over Skiddaw, so much so as to exclude many a height beyond it. Passing this mountain in our course to the south, we saw, immediately below, the fells around Derwentwater, the lake itself remaining still concealed in their deep, rocky bosom. Southward and westward, the whole prospect was a "turbulent chaos of dark mountains." All individual dignity was now lost in the immensity of the whole, and every variety of character was overpowered by that of astonishing and gloomy grandeur.

Over the fells of Borrowdale, and so far to the south, the northern end of Windermere appeared, like a wreath of grey smoke, that spreads along the mountain's side. More southward still, and beyond all the fells and the lakes, Lancaster sands extended to the faintly seen waters of the sea. Then to the west Duddon sands gleamed in a long line among the fells of High Furness. Immediately under the eye lay Bassenthwaite, surrounded by many ranges of mountains, invisible from below. We overlooked all these dark mountains, and saw green cultivated vales over the tops of lofty rocks, and other mountains over these vales in many ridges, whilst innumerable narrow glens were traced in all their windings and seen uniting behind the hills with others that also sloped upwards from the lake.

The air on this summit was boisterous, intensely cold, and difficult to be inspired, though the day was below warm and serene. It was dreadful to look down from nearly the brink of the point on which we stood, upon the lake of Bassenthwaite and over a sharp and separated ridge of rocks that, from below, appeared of tremendous height, but now seemed not to reach half way up Skiddaw; it was almost as if

> The precipitation might down stretch
> Below the beam of sight.

Under the lee of an heaped-up pile of slates, formed by the customary contribution of one from every visitor, we found an old man sheltered, whom we took to be a shepherd, but afterwards learned was a farmer, and, as people in this neighbourhood say, a " 'statesman," that is, had land of his own. He was a native, and still an inhabitant of an adjoining vale; but so laborious is the enterprise reckoned that, though he had passed his life within view of the mountain, this was his first ascent. He descended with us for part of our way, and then wound off towards his own valley, stalking amidst the wild scenery, his large figure wrapt in a dark cloak, and his steps occasionally assisted by a long iron pronged pike, with which he had pointed out distant objects.

In the descent it was interesting to observe each mountain below gradually re-assuming its dignity, the two lakes expanding into spacious surfaces, the many little valleys that sloped upwards from their margins recovering their variegated tints of cultivation, the cattle again appearing in the meadows, and the woody promontories changing from smooth patches of shade into richly tufted summits. At about a mile from the top a great difference was perceptible in the climate, which became comparatively warm, and the summer hum of bees was again heard among the purple heath.

We reached Keswick about four o'clock, after five hours passed in this excursion, in which the care of our guide greatly lessened the notion of danger.

A MOUNTAIN DELUGE.

On the Helvellyn range of mountains, on August 22nd, 1749, a most remarkable flood happened—caused by impestuous rains—which descended into the Vale of St. John, near the celebrated Castle rock, which tradition had that, if a traveller advances, certain genii who govern the place, by virtue of their supernatural arts and necromancy, did strip of all its beauties, and by enchantment transform the magic walls, and which is celebrated by Sir Walter Scott, in his " Bridal of Triermain, a lover's tale." The clouds discharged their torrents like a waterspout; the streams from the mountains uniting, at length became so powerful a body, as to rend up the soil, gravel, and stones, to a prodigious depth, and bear with them mighty fragments of rock; several cottages were swept away from the declivities where they had stood in safety for a century; the vale was deluged, and many of the inhabitants with their cattle were lost. A singular providence protected many lives: a little school where all the youths of the neighbourhood were educated, at the instant crowded with its flock, stood in the very line of one of these torrents; but the hand of God, in a miraculous manner, stayed a rolling rock, in the midst of its dreadful course, which would have crushed the whole tenement with its innocents; and by its stand, the floods divided, and passed on this hand and on that, insulating the school-house and leaving the pupils and their master, trembling at once for the dangers escaped and as spectators of the horrid havoc in the valley, and the tremendous floods which encompassed them on every side. It began with most terrible thunder and lightning, the preceding day having been extremely sultry; the inhabitants for two hours before the breaking of the cloud, heard a strange noise, like the wind blowing in the tops of high trees. It was thought at the time to have been caused by a large body of water, which, by the lightning incessantly rarifying the air, broke at once on the tops of the mountains and descended upon the valley below, which is about three miles long, half a mile broad, and lies nearly north and south, being closed on the east and west sides with prodigious high, steep, and rocky mountains. Legburthwaite Fells, on the east side, received almost the whole cataract, for the extent of water did not extend above a mile in length : it chiefly swelled four small brooks, but to so amazing a degree, that the largest of them, called Catchety Gill swept away a mill and other edifices in five minutes, leaving the places where they stood covered with fragments of rock and rubbish three or four yards deep, insomuch that one of the mill-stones has never yet been found. During the violence of the storm, the fragments of rock, which rolled down the mountain, choked up the whole course of this brook, but the water forcing its way through a shivery rock, formed a chasm four yards wide and about eight or nine deep. The brooks lodged such quantities of gravel and sand on the meadows, that they are irrecoverably lost. Many large pieces of rock were carried a considerable way into the fields, some larger than a team of ten horses could move, and one of them measuring nineteen yards about.

ECHOES OF THE LAKES AND MOUNTAINS.

The surprising echoes which the report of a cannon, a fowling piece, a key bugle, or a band of music will excite is something marvellous and beyond conception on Derwent Lake, of a calm summer or autumn evening, when the surface of the water is as placid as a mirror.

A visitor to the Lake District describes his impressions as follows. " Whilst we sat to regale, the barge put off from shore to a station where the finest echoes were to be obtained from the surrounding mountains. The vessel was provided with six brass cannon, mounted on swivels; on discharging one of these pieces the report was echoed from the opposite rocks, where, by reverberation, it seemed to roll from cliff to cliff and return through every cave and valley, till the decreasing tumult gradually died away upon the ear,

The instant it had ceased, the sound of every distant waterfall was heard; but for an instant only, for the momentary stillness was interrupted by the returning echo on the hills behind, where the report was repeated like a peal of thunder bursting over our heads, continuing for several seconds, flying from haunt to haunt, till once more the sound gradually declined;— again the voice of waterfalls possessed the interval,— till, to the right, the more distant thunder arose upon some other mountain, and seemed to take its way up every winding dell and creek, sometimes behind, on this side or on that, in wondrous speed, running its dreadful course. When the echo reached the mountains within the line and channel of the breeze, it was heard at once, on the right and left, at the extremities of the lake. In this manner was the report of every discharge re-echoed seven distinct times.

At intervals we were relieved from this entertainment, which consisted of a wondrous tumult and grandeur of confusion, by the music of two French horns, whose harmony was repeated from every recess which echo haunted on the borders of the lake;— here the breathings of the organ was imitated; there the bassoons with clarionets; in this place, from the harsher sounding cliffs, the cornet; in that, from the wooded creek, amongst the caverns and the waterfalls, we heard the soft-toned lute, accompanied with the languishing strains of enamoured nymphs: whilst in the copse and grove was still retained the music of the horns. All this vast theatre was possessed by innumerable ærial beings who breathed celestial harmony.

As we finished our repast, a general discharge of the guns roused us to new astonishment. Although we had heard with great surprise the former echoes, this exceeded them so much that it seemed incredible; for on every hand the sounds were reverberated and returned from side to side, so as to give the semblance of that confusion and horrid uproar, which the falling of these stupendous rocks would occasion, if, as by some internal combustion, they were rent to pieces and hurled into the lake.

At the present time, a cannon is kept at the Lodore Hotel, Derwentwater, which is fired, at a small cost, on request being made to the host, and the echoes produced by it in favourable weather are extraordinary, varying from nine to twelve distinct reverberations.

CHRISTMAS IN CUMBERLAND,

"No where," says Hone, in his Year Book (1832), "does the Christmas season produce more heart-inspiring mirth than among the inhabitants of Cumberland. The farmer may be seen with his hands enveloped in huge mittens, thrust half-way into his breeches pockets, and his fustian jacket buttoned well up under his chin, jogging merrily along to his daily labour, singing or whistling as he goes, whilst his jolly red face, scarcely perceivable on account of the dense fog, appears like 'the sun dimly seen through a mist.' The dairy-maid, with her 'geggin' (milk-pail) in her hand, hurries, shivering through the cold, to the 'byre' (cow-house), where the delightful smell and genial warmth of the cows which she sits down to milk, occasion her to observe—'it's worth while coming thro' t' snaw a' purpose to enjoy t' pleesur o' gittin' among t' byre.' This is contradicted: The lad who is 'mucking the byre,' and who is obliged to issue out at the door ever minute to throw the dirt from his 'muck-fork' on to t' 'midden' (dunghill) grumbles, and says 'she wadn't say sae, if she hed his wark t' du'; and she, of course, from some old grudge she has against him, is greatly pleased at his mortification.

"The frozen 'tarns' (small lakes or ponds may be seen covered with boys, some with wisps of straw brushing off the snow, others sliding in their wooden clogs, which are more convenient for this purpose than shoes. They, exhorting each other to 'keep the pot boiling,' till perhaps one of them falls, and the next, on account of the velocity, not being able to stop, stumbles over him; and so on, until most of them lie rolling in a heap together, to the great joy of their comrades, who cry out, 'my pot boils over,' and with all their might endeavour to prevent them from getting up. Sliding by moonlight is very common here, because the men, not having been able to leave work in the day time, think it a fine opportunity to enjoy their favourite amusement of 'shurlin.'

"On stepping into the 'laithe' (barn), we may there see two stout hearty fellows, opposite to each other, alternately belabouring the ground with their flails till it rings again, whilst the straw, chaff, and corn fly about in all directions. At intervals they stop to pay their respects to a brown jug in the corner, which contains either home-brewed ale or churned milk.

"In the farm-house we may find the good dame and her rosy-cheeked daughters busied in preparing mince-pies, raised pies, tarts, and other good things, which indicate that something particular is about to take place.

"In short, with Christmas eve commences a regular series of 'festivities and merry-makings.' Night after night, if you want the farmer or his family, you must look for them anywhere but at home, and in the different homes that you pass at one, two, or three in the morning—should you happen to be out so late—you will find candles and fires still unextinguished. At Christmas, every farmer gives two 'feasts,' one called 't' auld foaks' neet,' which is for those who are married, and the other 't' young foaks' neet,' for those who are single. Suppose you and I, sir, take the liberty of attending one of these feasts unasked (which by-the-bye is considered no liberty at all in Cumberland) and see what is going on. Upon entering the room we behold several card parties, some at 'whist,' others at 'loo' (there called 'lant') or any other game that may suit their fancy. You will be surprised on looking over the company to find that there is no distinction of persons. Masters and servants, rich and poor, humble and lofty, all mingle together without restraint; all cares are forgotten, and each one seems to glory in his own enjoyment and in that of his fellow creatures. It is pleasant to find ourselves in such society, especially as it is rarely in one's life that such opportunities offer. Cast your eyes towards the sideboard, and there see that large bowl of punch, which the good wife is pressing her guests to partake of, with apples, oranges, biscuits, and other agreeable eatables in plenty. The hospitable master welcomes us with a smiling countenance, and requests us to take seats and join one of the tables.

"In due time some one enters to tell the company that supper is waiting, thither we adjourn, and find the raised and mince pies, all sorts of tarts, and all cold, except the welcomes and *entrées*—with cream, ale, etc., in abundance; in the midst of all a large goose pie, which seems to say, 'cut and come again.'

"After supper, the party return to the card room, sit there for two or three hours longer, and afterwards make the best of their way home to 'take a good long nap,' and prepare for the same scene the next night. At these Cumberland feasts intoxication is entirely out of the question—it never happens."

THE ONLY CUMBERLAND MARTYR.

Cumberland had one native, who, going up to London, first found a husband, and then met with martyrdom. This was a woman, one Elizabeth Foster. She was born at Greystoke; her maiden surname was unknown. In London she was married to John

Foster, cutler, of the Parish of St. Bride, in Fleet-street, and being summoned before Bishop Bonner (of cruel memory) for not coming to church, was imprisoned, and strictly examined. Being moved by the Bishop to desert her answers, she replied: "I will not go from them by God's grace." Hereupon she was condemned, and in the fifty-fifth year of her age was burnt at Smithfield with six others, all in one fire, on January 27th, 1556.

CUMBERLAND MOSS-TROOPERS.

Fuller, in his "History of the Worthies of England," thus quaintly describes these troublesome people (1662):—"So strange the condition of their living, if considered in their *original, increase, height, decay*, and *ruine*.

"1. *Original.* I conceive them the same called borderers in Mr. Cambden, and charactered by him to be a wild and warlike people: they are called *Moss-Troopers*, because dwelling in the *mosses* and riding in *troops*. They dwell in the *bounds*, or meeting of two kingdomes, but obey the laws of neither. They come to church as seldome as the 29th of February comes into the kalendar.

"2. *Increase.* When England and Scotland were united in *Great Britain*, they that formerly lived by *hostile incursions* betook themselves to the robbing of their neighbours. Their sons are free of the trade by their fathers copy; they are like unto Job (not in *piety* and *patience*), but in sudden *plenty* and *poverty*; sometimes having *flocks* and *herds* in the morning, none at night, and perchance many again next day. They may give for their motto *vivitar ex rapta*, stealing from their honest neighbours what sometimes they regain. They are a nest of hornets—strike *one* and stir *all* of them about your ears. Indeed, if they promise safely to conduct a traveller, they will perform

G

it with the fidelity of a Turkish janizary, otherwise wo be to him that falleth into their quarters.

"3. *Height*, amounting forty years since to some thousands. These compelled the vicinage to purchase their security by paying a constant rent unto them. When in their greatest height they had two great enemies, the *laws of the land* and the *Lord William Howard* of *Naworth*. He sent many of them to *Carlisle*; to that place where the *officer always doth his work by daylight*. Yet these *Moss-Troopers*, if possibly they could procure the pardon for a condemned person of their company, would advance great sums out of their *common stock;* who, in such a case, *cast in their lots amongst themselves, and all have one purse.*

"4. *Decay*, caused by the wisdome, valour, and diligence of the Right Honourable *Charles* Lord *Howard* Earl of *Carlisle*, who routed these English Tories with his regiment. His severity unto them will not only be excused, but *commended* by the judicious, who consider how our great lawyer doth describe such persons who are solemnly outlaw'd. '*Thenceforward* [after they are outlaw'd] *they wear a* wolf's-head, *so that they lawfully may be destroyed without any judiciall inquisition, as who carry their own condemnation about them, and deservedly die without law because they refused to live according to law.*

5. *Ruine.* Such the success of this worthy Lord's severity that he made a *thorough reformation* amongst them, and the *ringleaders* being destroyed, the rest are reduced to *legall* obedience, and so I trust will continue."

AN UNFORTUNATE EARL OF CARLISLE.

In the reign of Edward II., Andreas de Harcla, born at Harcla, was created Earl of Carlisle for his eminent services at Boroughbridge, where he killed Humphrey Bohun, Earl of Hereford, and took Thomas

Plantagenet, Earl of Lancaster, with many others of the nobility, prisoners, and delivered them to the king. For his prowess in this battle, the Isle of Man was also bestowed upon him. "Next year," says Fuller, "I know not upon what discontentment, he fell into private confederacy with the king's foes, the Scots, for which he was taken and condemned. Now lest the nobility of others should by secret sympathy suffer, in his disgraceful death, the Earl was first parted from the Man, and his honour severed from his person, by a solemn degradation, having his knightly spurs hewed off from his heels, which done, he was hang'd, drawn, and quartered."

OLD CUMBERLAND PROVERBS.

"If Skiddaw hath a cap,
Scruffell wots full well of that."

"There are two neighbour hills," explains Fuller, in his "Worthies of England," "the one in the county, the other in Anandale, in Scotland. If the former be capp'd with clouds and foggy mists, it will not be long before rain falls on other."

"When thy neighbour's house doth burn,
Take heed the next be not thy turn."

Says Fuller on this proverb: "The Cumberlanders have found the truth hereof by their sad experience in our Civil Wars, paying dear for their vicinity with Scotland.

"Skiddaw, Llewellyn, and Carticand,
Are the highest hills in all England.

It is difficult to reconcile this rhyme with another which is met with in the same author (Cambden)—

"Ingleborrow, Pendle, and Penigent,
Are the highest hills between Scotland and Trent."

But in order of an expedient betwixt them, we may

observe, first, that every county is given to *magnify* (not to say *altify*) their own things therein. Secondly, that the survey goes according to the guess of men's eyes (as never exactly measured), variable according to several apprehensions. Thirdly, some hills are higher in view, rising almost perpendicularly all of a sudden by themselves, whilst the invisible greatness of others are not heeded so much : which mount with the country about them, creeping up insensibly by degrees.

BEN WELLS, THE WONDERFUL DANCING-MASTER.

The people of Westmorland and Cumberland, as is well known, are very fond of athletic exercises, and extraordinary powers are still developed among them. During the long life of Wordsworth in this region, there was one man more famous among the common folk than he, namely, Ben Wells, for fifty years dancing-master and fiddler to the country people of Cumberland. Ben was the kind of man who, in a more primitive time, gave country folk their legends. The instrument being changed, Ben might have been the original of the boy in "A Merry Geste of the Frere and the Boye," who had a magic pipe—

> "All that may the pipe here
> Shall not themselfe stere,
> But laugh and lepe about."

He not only made cows and milkmaids dance, but so wrought on a friar that he capered until bit by bit he lost

> "His cope and scapelary
> And all his other wede."

Mr. Craig Gibson, F.S.A., has written (1869) a lyric about Ben Wells in the Cumberland dialect, and in a note says :—" The last time I met him was about twenty years ago in the bar parlour of an inn in the southern part of the lake district, where the strains of his fiddle, produced at my request, caused such excitement that a general and very uproarious dance (of males only) set in, and was kept up with such energy that, the space being confined, the furniture was seriously damaged, and Ben was at last ejected by the landlady, as the readiest—indeed, the only— method of putting a stop to the riot. He was light, muscular, and springy, and in his earlier years wonderfully swift of foot, so much so, that the late Dr. Johnstone, of Cockermouth, told me that he once (at Scale Hill) saw him, without any assistance, run down and capture a wild rabbit—a proof of activity rarely paralleled." We here quote two verses of Mr. Gibson's poem upon this celebrated Cumberland character :—

> Ben Wales's fiddle many a neet
>   Gev weel-oiled springs to t' heaviest heels,
> For few cud whyet hod the'r feet
>   When Ben struck up his heartenin' reels.
> Wid elbow-room an' rozel't weel,
>   Swinge! how he'd mak fwoke kev an' prance,
> An' nowt cud match t' sly fiddle squeal
>   At' signal'd kiss i' t' cushion-dance.
>
> Fwokes ways turn different t' langer t' mair,
>   An' what lang sen, was reets grown wrang;
> We're meàst on us ower fine to care
>   For heàmly dance, teun, tiàl, or sang,
> An' nowte's meàd verra lastin' here ;
>   T' best bow-hand growes ould and fails,
> An' t' listest legs git num' an' queer.
>   Few last sa weel as auld Ben Wales.

THE GIANT OF TROUTBECK PARK.

Harriet Martineau's account of this giant is as follows :—" Tradition tells of a giant, a man of amazing strength, who lived in Troutbeck Park, in the time of Henry IV. He begged from house to house till he came there, but finding an empty dwelling he took possession. This house had been forfeited to the

Crown, and was of so little value that he remained for a time undisturbed. At last a tenant was found, and came to take possession; but the giant, who was quite uncivilised, and knew no law but strength, prevented him. Upon this he was sent to London, where he so pleased the king by his feats of strength that he was promised anything he might ask for. His petition was the house in Troutbeck Park, the paddock behind it to get peat for fuel, and liberty to cut wood in Troutbeck Park. It is said that the king asked him what he lived upon, and his reply was, 'Thick pottage and milk, that a mouse might walk upon dry shod, for breakfast, and the sunny side of a wedder for his dinner when he could get it' (*i.e.* the whole of the wether). His mother lived with him, and they toiled on these hill-sides, making a livelihood chiefly by cutting and burning the common brackens (ferns), from which they obtained a residue which was used in the manufacture of soap. Their graves are said to be discernible near the old Log-house! This was the estate afterwards given by Charles I. to Huddlestone Phillipson for his services in the civil wars." He was known by the name of Hugh Hird. Among other traditions about this giant, one relates: that alone with his bow and arrows he drove back a party of Scotch marauders.

THE "MORTAL MAN" INN.

Somewhat beyond Hogarth's house at Troutbeck stands a memorable inn with the sign of the "Mortal Man." It was said to have had a curious old sign, representing two men, one fat and jolly, the other haggard, with an appropriate four rhyming lines beneath. But this sign has long since disappeared. The inn is now kept by one Isaac Walker, a solid, sensible, honest specimen of a Westmorland yeoman, and one who knew full well the value of the old sign could he have got it. Isaac had preserved with the greatest care every antique thing about the old inn, such as an oak cupboard (300 years old) in the wall, and some letters on the outside wall, with date " I. C., 1689." The initials are those of Isaac Cookson, and Isaac Walker's mother was a Cookson. The landlord is fond of repeating the correct version of the lines which were on the sign from which the inn derived its name :—

> " Thou Mortal Man, that lives on bread,
> What is't that makes thy nose so red?
> Thou silly ass, that looks so pale,
> It is by drinking Sally Birkett's ale."

" It's an old Troutbeck riddle for strangers," Isaac would say to his visitors, " that small as the village seems, it has 300 bulls, constables, and bridges. The township was divided into three parts, called 'hundreds' and each had a constable, a bull, and a bridge. But old things go. We haven't ghosts now-a-days—Troutbeck railway station's too near. I can remember when a boy would run fit to break his neck past an old lime kiln near this, because of a ghost. Somebody murdered there by being thrown into the kiln. But there are very few superstitions among us now; and the fewer the better."

HOGARTH'S FATHER'S HOUSE.

Hogarth the painter's ancestors resided in Troutbeck village. The uncle of that great artist resided here, and was famous in the neighbourhood for his songs. These were satirical, humorous, and generally about his neighbours. The house of Hogarth's uncle is still standing in the village, and near it two old trees he is said to have planted. It is a dwelling not mean, but uniquely commonplace there; for the houses of Troutbeck are rather striking, having many gables, and pretty porticoes made of slate stone. The house where the Hogarth's would have lived, is now that of Mr. George Browne, and contains much quaint old furniture. This charming cottage with its chimneys transformed into ivy towers, and its walls set with Queen Anne windows, framed in climbing-roses and morning glories, would drive a London pre-Raphaelite " mad with sweet desire."

WORDSWORTH AT HOME.

When Isaac Walker (landlord of the " Mortal Man " inn at Troutbeck) was a lad he lived in the service of William Wordsworth, and thus quaintly describes the poet, of whom he was very fond and proud:—" I was put out to service in a family at Ambleside, and when my master and mistress wanted to travel away in foreign countries, they asked Mr. Wordsworth to take me just to keep me out of mischief. So I staid in his service at Rydal about a year. Mr. Wordsworth was a plain-looking man, with thin face and large features, especially a pretty big nose. He lived very plainly. He had not a bit of pride and would talk familiarly but gravely with servants. He use to talk with me kindly and familiarly, and I had a warm affection for him. He liked to be out of doors whenever he could. Sometimes he was picking up things to look at them, and then he was talking to things in a very queer way. I can see him now: following a bumble-bee all over the garden; he puts his hands behind him this way, and then bends over towards the bee, and wherever it went he followed, making a noise like it—' Boom-oom-oom-oom.' " (Isaac Walker would here imitate the action and the sound perfectly, but said he could never get the bees' sound so rich as Mr. Wordsworth had it.) " He would stick to that bee," Isaac continued, " long and long, until it went away; you might go away and come back, and still you would see him striding after that bee, with his mouth down towards it, and hear his 'Boom-oom-oom. But there was nothing he didn't take notice of. I don't remember so well his friends who used to come and see him; the one I remember most was Mr. Hartley Coleridge, who was a little fellow—carried his head on one side. I remember well Professor Wilson; he was a splendid man, very active and strong. 'The Mortal Man' was his favourite inn over here; but that was before my time. I was sorry to leave Rydal Mount when the time came."

A GREAT BULL FIGHT.

All the wars of Cæsar have hardly so large a place in their traditions as a certain famous contest between a Troutbeck bull and an Orrest Head bull. Josiah Browne of the latter place had a tremendous bull, and some man at Troutbeck had another, and there was so much brag on each side that it was agreed to have a fight between the animals. The terms were that the winner should have the fallen animal, and that they were to meet half way between the two places It was a tremendous battle. The whole country for many miles around gathered, and Josiah came riding on the back of his monster. The Troutbeck bull was prodigious, and fought furiously; the struggle was like hills hurled against each other, and shook the earth. Finally, the Troutbeck animal fell, and Josiah Browne, having presented it to the poor of Troutbeck, rode back on his victorious bull to Orrest Head. It is safe to say that Rome in her palmiest days never had such a combat as that.

THE CUSHION DANCE.

This dance is peculiar to Cumberland, and is the finishing dance of a rural ball or merry night, and is thus performed. A young man, carrying a cushion, paces round the room in time to an appropriate tune, selects a girl, lays the cushion at her feet, and both kneel upon it and kiss, the fiddler making an extraordinary squeal during the operation. The girl then takes the cushion to another young man, who kisses her as before, and leaves her free to "link" with the first, and march round the room. This is repeated till the whole party is brought in, when they all form a circle, and "kiss out" in the same manner, sometimes varying it by the kissers sitting on two chairs, back to back, in the middle of the ring, and kissing over their shoulders—a trying process to bashful youth of either sex.

MRS. HEMANS' HOME ON WINDERMERE.

This gifted woman in 1830 paid a visit to William Wordsworth, and was so enchanted with lake scenery and solitude that for some time she made and called her picturesque tree-embowered cottage, "Dove Nest." Here the sweet poetess sought repose in her declining years; and thus she apostrophises the locality of her home :—

> O vale and lake, within your mountain urn,
> Smiling so tranquilly, and set so deep!
> Oft doth your dreamy loveliness return,
> Colouring the tender shadows of my sleep
> With light Elysian; for the hues that steep
> Your shores in melting lustre, seem to float
> On golden clouds from spirit-lands remote—
> Isles of the blest—and in our memory keep
> Their place with holiest harmonies.

In one of her letters she thus alludes to "Dove's Nest":—"I am writing to you from an old-fashioned alcove in the little garden, round which the sweetbriar and the rose tree have completely run wild; and I look down from it upon lovely Windermere, which seems at this moment even like another sky, so truly is every summer cloud and tint of azure pictured in its transparent mirror. I am so delighted with the spot that I scarcely know how I shall leave it. The situation is one of the deepest retirement; but the bright lake before me, with all its fairy barks and sails, glancing like things of life over its blue water, prevents the solitude from being overshadowed by anything like sadness."

But however much she loved the place it was not her destiny to die here. At the early age of 41 she died in Dublin, and was there interred in St. Anne's Church. Over her grave were inscribed some lines from one of her own dirges :—

>Calm on the bosom of thy God,
> Fair spirit, rest thee now;
>Even while with us thy footsteps trod,
> His seal was on thy brow.

>Dust, to its narrow home beneath;
> Soul, to its place on high;
>They that have seen thy look in death
> No more may fear to die.

BORROWDALE EAGLE STORIES.

There is a succession of wild and romantic scenes in the gorge of Borrowdale. Grange, a small village, is delightfully situate on the west side of the river Derwent, about a mile above its entrance into the lake. It is about four miles from Keswick. Here Banks, the philosopher, was born. Castle-crag, under which lies this sweet village, appears in the centre of an amphitheatre of mountains threatening to block up the pass into Borrowdale. The Saxons in turn occupied the fortress, and it was given with all Borrowdale to the Monks of Furness. The *Grange* was the place where they laid up their grain, and also the salt they made at a salt spring, of which works there are still some vestige below Grange.

Grey, the poet, speaks with complacency of the hospitality of a young farmer at Grange, in whose house he enjoyed a repast of milk, oaten cakes and ale. This farmer, he says, was "the man that last year plundered the eagle's eyrie; all the dale are up in arms on such an occasion, for they lose abundance of lambs yearly, not to mention hares, partridges, grouse, &c. He was let down from the cliff in ropes to the shelf of the rock on which the nest was built, the people above shouting and hallooing to frighten the old birds, which flew screaming around but did not dare to attack him. He brought off the eaglet (for there is hardly more than one and an addle egg). The nest was roundish and more than a yard over. Seldom a year passes but they take the brood or eggs, and sometimes they shoot one, sometimes the other parent; but the survivor has always found a mate, (probably in Ireland) and they breed near the old place."

No bird has stronger feelings than the eagle. They are most faithful and affectionate. One mate till death, and one, two, or three eaglets in the eyry generally constitute all the precious family of the imperial bird.

The rocky scenes in Borrowdale, where the eagle took up his abode, are most fantastic, and the entrance rugged. One rock elbows out and turns the road directly against another. Here the Derwent, rapid as the Rhone, rolls its crystal streams through all the labyrinth of embattled obstacles. Indeed the scenes here are sublimely terrible, the assemblage of magnificent objects so stupendously great, and the arrangement so extraordinary curious, that they must excite the most sensible feelings of wonder and surprise, and at once impress the mind with reverential awe and admiration.

The most gigantic mountains that form the outline of this tremendous landscape, and include Borrowdale, are Eagle-crag, Glaramara, Bull-crag, and Serjeant-crag. On the front of the first, the bird of Jove formerly had his annual nest.

> "Here his dread seat the royal bird hath made
> To awe the inferior subjects of the shade,
> Secure he built it for a length of days.
> Impervious, but to Phoebus' piercing rays;
> His young he trains to eye the solar light
> And soar beyond the fam'd Icarian flight."

But, even here, the monarch of the air was not safe from the pursuit of man; for in this rocky region were found men who, at great peril to life and limb, were let down, by means of a strong cord, some twenty fathoms or more, to the ledge on which the eagles built their nests. In one hand he carried his iron-headed mountain staff, with which he warded off the frequent and ferocious attacks of the parent birds; while, with the other, he clung tightly to the slender cord that, to him, separated life from death. Ultimately the brave shepherd usually managed to gain a footing on the slender ledge, and a sickening spectacle presented itself to his view: strewed about in all directions were the remnants of half-eaten lambs, hares, moor game, and ducks, the effluvia of which absolutely thickened the air. Once landed on the ledge, the shepherd commenced to ravage the eyry of its eggs, or the young eaglets, if there were any. If he brought the young ones away alive, he had the birds for his trouble and risk; if the eggs, his neighbour shepherds gave him five shillings for each egg. When the adventurer failed, then the eaglets were reared, and as soon as strong enough were taken away by the parent birds to some other spot, there to carry on their work of destruction on their own account amongst the shepherds' flocks.

The eagles which gave their name to the crag in Borrowdale, being disturbed by the proceedings just described, settled themselves on a rock at Seathwaite, and afterwards crossed the ridge into Eskdale. One of these eagles once carried off a large sheep dog, but the dog's master espying him, immediately let the bird have the contents of his gun. The shot took effect, but not before a piece of flesh was torn from the dog's neck. The eagle vanished, but was found a week afterwards on the uplands of Seatoller nearly starved. Its bill had been split by the shot, and its tongue was set fast in the cleft; it could not make much resistance, and was carried home captive. But when relieved and restored, it became so violent that it was necessarily killed. Its mate brought a successor from a distance, a much smaller bird, and of a different species. They built however, for fourteen more years in Borrowdale, before they flew over to Eskdale. They were not long left in peace there; and when the larger bird was at length shot, his mate disappeared entirely.

"Such devastation," says Harriet Martineau, "as was caused by these birds is not heard of now; but while there are crags aloft, and lambs in the vales, there will be more or fewer, nobler or nearer, birds of prey. Three gentlemen—two of whom were travelled men and not likely to be mistaken in such a matter —declare that, in 1850, they saw one sweep down Scandale Fell into Kirkstone Pass, and rest on a crag in the vale, some way above Brother's Water. There is, however, a preponderance of disbelief of there being now any nest or settlement of eagles among the mountains of Westmorland and Cumberland.

RAYRIGG—THE LAKE RESIDENCE OF WILLIAM WILBERFORCE

Three quarters of a mile from Bowness is Rayrigg, which has more to recommend it to public attention than even its own beautiful scenery for it was here that the illustrious Wilberforce, the champion of freedom to the slave, made his residence whenever he could escape from his Parliamentary duties. Bowness is the port of Windermere, and here the little lake steamboats now put up. The most venerable objects in this place, are the old churchyard with its dark yews, and the church, long and low.

> "Not raised in nice proportions was the pile,
> But large and massy ; for duration built ;
> With pillars crowded, and the roof upheld
> By naked rafters intricately cross'd,
> Like leafless underboughs, 'mid some thick grove
> All wither'd by the depth of shade above."

The chancel window of the church contains very fine painted glass from Furness Abbey. The rectory, which is hardly less venerable than the church, stands at a considerable distance from the village, and is approached through fields and a garden. The old-fashioned porch is there, of which this is said to be the last remaining instance in the whole district,—the roomy, substantial porch, with benches on each side, long enough to hold a little company of parishioners, and a round ivy-clad chimney immediately surmounting the porch. Rayrigg, in the immediate vicinity, as we have said, was the residence of William Wilberforce, and for that reason is looked upon with reverence by every pilgrim to these romantic shores. By some it is said to resemble Voltaire's Mansion of Ferney, on the Lake of Geneva. In 1788, the last year of Wilberforce's residence in this beautiful spot, he writes to a friend :—" I never enjoyed the country more than during this visit, when, in the early morning, I used to row out alone, and find an oratory under one of the woody islands in the middle of the lake."

He repeatedly invited his friend, William Pitt, to share for a few weeks, or even days, the delights of a country life with him here, but the Premier was invariably prevented by the all-absorbing duties of his high station, from taking the relaxation which he would have enjoyed so much.

THE POET GRAY'S BEAUTIFUL DESCRIPTION OF GRASMERE.

The author of the "Elegy in a Country Churchyard," the finest poem in the English language, in a letter to a friend (1765) thus delightfully describes Grasmere on his visit to the Lakes. Nothing can exceed the beauty and finish of this miniature picture of this beautiful spot, much as has since been written upon it. In his country tours the poet carried with him a plano-convex mirror, which, in surveying landscapes gathers into one confined glance the forms and tints of the surrounding scene. In the letter referred to he says: "Passed by the little chapel of Wiborn, out of which the Sunday Congregation were then issuing. Passed a beck [rivulet] near Dunmail Raise, and entered Westmorland a second time; now began to see Helmcrag, distinguished from its rugged neighbours, not so much by its height as by the strange broken outline of its top, like some gigantic building demolished, and the stones that composed it flung across each other in wild confusion. Just beyond it opens one of the sweetest landscapes that art ever attempted to imitate. The bosom of the mountains here spreading into a broad basin, discovers in the midst *Grasmere Water;* its margin is hollowed into 'small bays, with eminences, some of rock some of soft turf,' that half conceal and vary the figure of the little lake they command From the shore a low promontory pushes itself into the water; and on it stands a white village, with a parish church rising in the midst of it, having enclosures, corn-fields, and meadows, green as an emerald, with trees, and hedges, and cattle, fill up the whole space from the edge of the water; and just opposite to you is a large farm-house, at the bottom of a steep smooth lawn, embosomed in old woods, which climb half-way up the mountain sides, and discover above a broken line of crags that crown the scene. Not a single red tile, no staring gentleman's house breaks in upon the repose of this unsuspected paradise; but all is peace, rusticity and happy poverty, in its sweetest, most becoming attire."

Such was Grasmere when the poet visited it a century ago.

> Tranquil and shut out
> From all the strife that shakes a jarring world.

But now its solitude has given place to the busy hum of human life coming and going—hotels, lodging-houses, and coaches.

TWO ANCIENT CUMBERLAND BALLADS.

1.—GUID STRANG YELL.

Our Ellek likes fat bacon weel,
    And haver-bannock pleases Dick;
A cowd-lword meks lal Wully fain,
    And cabbish aye turns Philip sick.
Our deame's for gurdle-ceake and tea,
    And Betty's aw for thick pez-keale;
Let ilk you fancy what he wull,
    Still my delight is guid strang yell.
I ne'er had muckle, ne'er kent want,
    Ne'er wrang'd a neybor, frien, or kin,
My wyfe and bairns 'buin aw I prize,
    There's music i' their varra din:
I labour suin, I labour leate,
    And chearfu' eat my humble meal;
My weage can feed and clead us aw
    And whiles affords me guid strang yell.
What's aw the warld without content?
    Wi' that and health man can't be peer;
We suin slip off frae friends and foes,
    Then wher but fuils wad feght for geer.
'Bout kings and consuls gowks may fratch;
    For me I scworn to vex mysel',
But laugh at courts and ower-grown knaves,
    When I've a hush o' guid strang yell.

2.—THE DISAPPOINTED.

This ancient ballad differs from the foregoing inasmuch as it is an expression of a true love of the human heart, rather than the bacchanalian one for the love of "Guid strang yell." It breathes a sincere and unselfish maiden's love for a cheerful honest swain:—

> The muin shone breet at nine last neet,
> When Jemmy Sharp cam o'er the muir;
> Weel did I ken a lover's fit,
> And heard him softly tap the duir:
> My fadder started i' the nuik,
> "Rin, Jenny! see what's that?" he said;
> I whispered, "Jemmy come to mworn,"
> And then a leame excuse fain meade.
> I went to bed but could'nt sleep,
> This luive sae breaks a body's rest,
> The mwornin dawn'd, then up I gat,
> And seegh'd and aye luik'd towards the west,
> But when, far off, I saw the wood
> Where he unlock'd his heart to me,
> I thaught o' mony a happy hour,
> And then a tear gush'd frae my e'e.
> To neet my fadder's far frae heame,
> And wonnet come this three hours yet;
> But O, it pours, and I'd be leath
> That Jemmy sud for me get wet!
> Yet, if he dis, guid heame-brew'd yell
> Will warm his cheerfu' honest heart;
> Wi' him, my verra life o' life,
> I's fain to meet, but leath to part.

MISS MARTINEAU'S DESCRIPTION OF PROFESSOR WILSON.

The Westmorland home of Professor Wilson (better known as "Christopher North") was at Elleray, one of the attractions round and about Windermere. Here Wilson came after his University career, and spent a merry life; and here he brought his bride in 1811. The last of the Professor's servants, "Old James Newby," the gardener, held his post at the old cottage under the tree until 1869. Billy Balmer, the Professor's favourite boatman, and others, had gone some years before. Observe the fine old sycamore, about which the enthusiastic Professor says: "Never in this well wooded world, not even in the days of the Druids, could there have been such another tree! It would be easier to imagine two Shakspeares. Yet I have heard people say it is far from being a large tree. A small one it cannot be, with a house in its shadow—an unawakened house, that looks as if it were dreaming. True, 'tis but a cottage, a Westmorland cottage. But then it has several roofs shelving away there in the lustre of the loveliest lichens; each roof with its own assortment of doves and pigeons preening their pinions in the morning pleasance. O, sweetest and shadiest of all sycamores, we love thee beyond all other trees."

"It is probable," says Harriet Martineau, "that no one sees Storrs Pier without thinking of Professor Wilson; and, indeed, there is no spot in the neighbourhood with which his memory and the gratitude of his readers is not associated. Anywhere such a presence is rarely seen; and it was especially impressive in the places he best loved to haunt. More than one person has said that Wilson reminded them of the first man, Adam; so full was his large frame of vitality, force, and sentience. His tread seemed to shake the ground, and his glance to pierce through stone walls; and, as for his voice, there was no heart that could stand before it. In his hours of emotion he swept away all hearts whithersoever he would. Not less striking was it to see him in a mood of repose, as he was seen when steering the packet-boat that used to pass between Bowness and Ambleside, before the steamers were put upon the lake. Sitting motionless, with his hand upon the tiller, in the presence of journeymen and market women, his eye apparently looking beyond everything into nothing, and his mouth closed above his beard, as if he meant never to speak again; he was quite as impressive and immortal an image as he could have been to the students of his moral philosophy class or the comrades of his

jovial hours. He was known, and with reverence
and affection, beside the trout stream, and the mountain tarn, and amidst the deep gloom of Elleray,
where he could not bring himself to let a sprig be
lopped that his wife had loved. Every old boatman
and young angler, every hoary shepherd and primitive
dame among the hills of the district, knew him and
enjoyed his presence. He made others happy by
being intensely happy himself when his brighter moods
were on him, and when he was mournful no one
desired to be gay. He has gone with his joy and his
grief; and the region is so much darker in a thousand
eyes."

THE GIANT'S GRAVE.
(A REMARKABLE MONUMENT OF ANTIQUITY IN PENRITH CHURCHYARD).

Penrith Church was rebuilt in 1722; it is a fine
structure, distinguished by a neat and elegant simplicity. In the churchyard is a remarkable monument
of antiquity; it consists of two upright pillars of stone,
about ten feet in height and fifteen feet asunder,
standing in a direction east and west; on each side
are two others of a semicircular form, placed edgewise
in the ground. This monument is most likely a
sepulchral monument, but whether its origin is to be
attributed to the British, Saxons, Romans, or Danes,
is not agreed upon by antiquaries. Pennant says:—
"'These stones seem to have been monumental, and
are evidently Christian, as appears on the cross in the
capital; fable says that they were to perpetuate the
memory of Cæsanius, a hero of gigantic stature, whose
body extended from stone to stone; but it is probable
that the space marked by these columns contained
several bodies, or might have been a family sepulchre."
These conjectures, however, do not appear to be well
supported. The name of the " Giant's Grave." which

this singular monument has retained through a succession of ages, and the rude sculpture upon one part of it rather favours the traditionary story that it is the tomb of Sir Hugh Cæsarius, a man of great courage, who was successful in clearing the forest of Inglewood from the ferocious wild boars that in those remote times infested the neighbouring country. In an age when the stature of a hero was magnified by popular credulity, in proportion to the danger and magnitude of his enterprises, it is not surprising that this valorous knight, who, perhaps, might somewhat exceed the common size, was exalted into a giant. Sandford, in his manuscript account, written about the conclusion of the 16th century, relates that he was told by Mr. Page, who was schoolmaster at Penrith from 1581 to 1591, that a strange gentleman desired to have some of the principal inhabitants to sup with him, whereupon Mr. Page and some others attended him. The stranger told them that he came to see the antiquities of the place; and, drawing out a paper, said that Sir Hugh Cæsarius had a hermitage somewhere thereabouts called "Sir Hugh's parlour," and this place was sometime afterwards opened by one William Turner, who there found the great long shank bones of a man, and a broad sword. Not far from this monument stands a pillar called the "Giant's thumb," about six feet high and fourteen inches broad at bottom, the use and design of which have not been discovered.

ANCIENT USES OF BLACKLEAD OR WAD DISCOVERED IN A MINE IN BORROWDALE, NEAR KESWICK.

This mine was discovered near Keswick about 1710. In those days it was a mineral very scarce and not elsewhere to be met with. Camden in his History of England, calls it "That mineral earth or hard shining stone, which painters use in drawing their lines and shading their pieces in black and white.

Mr. Robinson in his Natural History of Cumberland and Westmorland say:—" Its composition is a black, pinguid, and shining earth impregnated with lead and antimony. Its natural uses are both mechanical and medicinal. It is a present remedy for the colic; it easeth the pain of gravel, stone, and stranguary; and for these and the like uses it is much sought up by apothecaries and physicians, who understand more of its medicinal uses than I am able to give account of. The manner of the country people's using it is thus:—First, they beat it small into meal, and then take as much of it in white wine or ale, as will lie upon a sixpence, or more, if the distemper require it. It operates by urine, sweat and vomiting. This account I had from those who had frequently used it in their distempers with good success. Besides those uses that are medicinal, it hath many other uses which increase the value of it. At the first discovery of it, the neighbourhood made no other use of it, but for marking their sheep; but is now made use of to glaze and harden crucibles and other vessels made of earth or clay, that are to endure the hottest fire; and, to that end it is wonderfully effectual, which much enhanceth the price of such vessels. By rubbing it upon iron arms, as guns, pistols, and the like, and tinging of them with its colour, it preserves 'them from' bursting. It is made use of by dyers of cloth, making their blues to stand unalterable. This mundic ore, having little of sulphur in its composition will not flow without a violent heat. It produceth a white regulus shining like silver. It cannot be made malleable."

The discovery of this blacklead or wad mine about Keswick, subsequently became of that importance that a special Act of Parliament was framed to protect them.

In the Act of Parliament 25 Geo. 2. c. 10, making it felony to break into any mine or wad, hole of wad or black cawke, commonly called blacklead, or to steal any from thence; there is a recital that the seam hath been discovered in one mountain or ridge of hills only in this realm, and that it hath been found by experience to be necessary for divers useful purposes, and more particularly in the casting of bomb-shells, round shot, and cannon balls."

A poet a century ago thus alludes to this famous mine :—

> " Southward, at distance, see the winding vale
> And rugged mountains of old Borrowdale
> Whose Black Lead Mine is fam'd through many a coas
> Nor can whole Europe such another boast.
> Here the first mountains past, new mountains rise
> And mountains still behind outbrave the skies ;
> Adown the rocks, hark how the torrent roars ;
> And noisy cascades fill the distant shores."

SIR WALTER SCOTT'S MEMORABLE VISIT TO THE LAKES.

In 1825 the illustrious novelist and poet on his return from Ireland, paid a visit to the hospitable house of Mr. Bolton at Storr's Hall on Lake Windermere and met with a gay reception. At this meeting not only Sir Walter Scott and Professor Wilson, but George Canning and William Wordsworth were present. "There was," says Mr. Lockhart (Scott's son-in-law and distinguished biographer) " high discourse intermingled with as gay feastings of courtly wit as ever Canning displayed, and a plentiful allowance on all sides of those airy transient pleasantries in which the fancy of poets, however wise and grave, delights to run riot, when they are sure not to be misunderstood. The weather was as Elysian as the scenery. There were brilliant cavalcades through the woods in the mornings, and delicious boatings on the Lake by moonlight, and the last day the Admiral of the Lake presided over one of the most splendid regattas that ever enlivened Windermere. Perhaps there were not fewer than fifty barges following in the Professor's* radiant procession when it paused at the point of Storr's to admit Mr. Bolton and his guests. The bards of the Lakes (Wordsworth and Wilson) led the cheers that hailed Scott and Canning, and music and sunshine, flags, streamers, and gay dresses, the merry hum of voices, and the rapid splashing of innumerable oars, made up a dazzling mixture of sensations as the flotilla wound its way among the richly foliaged islands, and along bays and promontories peopled into enthusiastic spectators."

"How soon, alas!" reflects Charles Mackay, "was the scene to darken for the two most celebrated actors in this splendid scene! Canning, even at that time, as Scott afterwards remarked, looking old, and haggard, and careworn, and so soon to die; and Scott himself was at the culminating point of his worldly prosperity;—already upon the descent: the cloud gathering upon his glory, and the darkness coming, in which he could not work." Canning lived but two years after the gay scene and Sir Walter seven. Mr. and Mrs. Bolton are gone, and Professor Wilson himself has followed "To that bourne from whence no traveller returns."

MODERN USE OF THE WORD "LAKE."

About thirty years ago there were not perhaps half-a-dozen persons in Keswick who knew what the word *Lake* meant, though *Lakes* and *Lake Poets* have latterly attracted so much of the attention of the world. It was then either called *Daran* (that is, Derwent), or *Keswick-Water*, but it now seldom

---

* The late Professor Wilson.

receives any other name than the *Lake*, and that of *Daran* is scarcely known.

The following dialogue between a mother and daughter, which Mr. Clarke (an authority on the subject) states to have been actually heard by him, affords a good illustration of this assertion, and is valuable at the same time as a specimen of the dialect of the natives.

Daughter: Oh! moother, moother, an ye hed been thear, ye wad ha stay'd tew; seck fine wark ye never saw. Efter dinner, we went to th' lake.

Mother: Lake! eigh thou wad lake an ramp and rive o' the cleighs I war'n. Let's luik if nin o' them be roven? What lake wast? Tennis or Anthony Blindman?

Daughter: Moother, ye dunt understund ma. Went to th' watter, and got ontuet in a booat; at hed things, like a battelter on aither side ont, at carried it on some way or other; an we drank finest stuff at ever was, they cawt it *cine* an *wider*.

Mother: Cine and wider, uman, what's tatt?

Daughter: What's tatt? Nay, I knaw nut.

Mother: What is't like?

Daughter: Like, it like? Like, it's like!—nay, I knaw nut what it's like; it's like whey-whig and *drink*, but far finer.

Mother: Hang the cine and wider, and the lakes; an thou hasn't roven the cleighs, nor worn the stocking heels out, I kair nut. Gitt te cloggs on, an doff that fine gown, and ligg by the hatt, an aw things; thou mun full muck to mworn, or gang toth' moss for this skelpin to-day; it's far better for tha.

Daughter: O, moother, yon talear, Gweardy, is a canny fellow.

Mother: Gitt away with the an thy canny fellow.*

---

* EXPLANATION.—*Cloggs*, shoes with thick wooden soles, armed at the heels and toes, with plates of iron called cawkers; *yan*, one; *mud*, must; *gang*, go; *dud seah*, did so; *wud*, would;

ha, have; *seck*, such; *wark*, work; *efter*, after; *evh*, yea; *lake*, in the north of England means playing; *rive o' the cleighs*, tear all thy clothes; I war'n, *warrant* or *suppose;* *luik*, look; *nin*, none; *roven*, torn; *ontuet*, upon it; *booat*, boat; *hed*, had; *battelter*, a piece of wood made not much unlike an oar, about four feet long. which the country people beat their linen with when they wash and bleach it; *carrit it on*, moved the boat in a manner she could not understand; *cawt*, called; *cine and wider*, meant for wine and cyder; *uman*, woman; *tatt*, that; *nut*, not; *whey-whig*, a liquor made of whey, into which is put mint, balm, walnut leaves, &c., which, when properly managed, drinks pleasantly in summer; *I kair not*, I care not; *ligg*, lay, *aw*, all; *mun*, must; *muck*, dung; *to-mworn*, to-morrow; *toth' moss*, the place where peat fuel is dug; *skelpin*, jumping— romping; *tha*, thou; O moother! *yon talear Gwearay is a canny fellow*, O, mother, tailor George is a pretty or handsome fellow.

DR. BROWN'S PICTURESQUE DESCRIPTION OF KESWICK.

The principal place in this large parish, Crosthwaite, in Allerdale-below-Derwent, is the market town of Keswick. The late Dr. Brown (a century ago) in a letter to a friend, describes it in the following elegant and very picturesque manner, and which, to our thinking, stands out for its force and beauty from all other descriptions. He says :—

"In my way to the north, I passed through Dovedale, and to say the truth, was disappointed in it. When I came to Buxton, I visited another or two of their romantic scenes; but these are inferior to Dovedale. They are but poor miniatures of KESWICK, which exceeds them more in grandeur than I can give you to imagine; and more, if possible, in beauty than in grandeur.

"Instead of the narrow slip of valley which is seen at Dovedale, you have at Keswick a vast amphitheatre, in circumference about twenty miles. Instead of a meagre rivulet, a noble living lake, ten miles round, of an oblong form, adorned with a variety of wooded islands. The rocks, indeed, of Dovedale are finely wild, pointed, and irregular, but the hills are both little and unanimated, and the margin of the brook is poorly edged with weeds, morass, and brushwood. But at Keswick you will, on one side of the lake, see a rich and beautiful landscape of cultivated fields, rising to the eye in fine inequalities, with noble groves of oak happily dispersed, and climbing the adjacent hills, shade above shade, in the most varied and picturesque forms. On the opposite shore you will find rocks and cliffs of stupendous height, hanging broken over the lake in horrible grandeur, some of them 1,000 feet high, the woods climbing up their steep and shaggy sides, where mortal foot never yet approached. On these dreadful heights the eagles build their nests. A variety of waterfalls are seen pouring from their summits, and tumbling in vast sheets from rock to rock in rude and terrible magnificence; while on all sides of this immense amphitheatre the lofty mountains rise round, piercing the clouds in shapes as spiry and fantastic as the very rocks of Dovedale. To this I must add the frequent and bold projection of the cliffs into the lake, forming noble bays and promontories. In other parts they finally retire from it and often open in abrupt chasms or clefts, through which at hand you see rich and cultivated vales, and beyond these, at various distances, mountain rising over mountain, among which new prospects present themselves in mist, till the eye is lost in an agreeable perplexity

"' Where active fancy travels beyond sense,
 And pictures things unseen.'

"Were I to analyse the two places into their constituent principles, I should tell you that the full perfection of Keswick consists of three circumstances *beauty, horror,* and *magnificence* united, the second of which is alone found in Dovedale; of *beauty* it hath little, nature having left it almost a desert; neither its small extent nor the diminutive and lifeless form of the hills admit *magnificence*. But to give you a complete idea of these three perfections, as they are joined in Keswick, would require the united powers of Claude, Salvator, and Pouissin. The first should throw his delicate sunshine over the cultivated vales, the scattered cots, the groves, the lake and wooded islands; the second should dash out the horror of the rugged cliffs, the steeps, the hanging woods, and foaming waterfalls; while the grand pencil of Pouissin should crown the whole with the majesty of the impending mountains."

THE TOURIST AND HIS DOG.

According to an ordnance survey, Helvellyn is 3,055 feet above the level of the sea, and from its summit extensive views are obtained of the most beautiful portions of the lakes. The report of these views have a bewitching sound to the ears of tourists, and while most are too timid to make the ascent (on foot or horseback) some have been bold enough to defy the perils of the way. The road ascends by Swirrel Edge, a rocky projection of Helvellyn, crowned by a conical hill, called Catchedicam, from which point a scramble of twenty minutes will place the adventurous traveller on the highest peak of Helvellyn.

"Some persons," says Dr. Mackay in his "English Lakes," "are bold enough in making the ascent to traverse the giddy and dangerous height of Striding Edge, but this road, says the "Bard of the Lakes" (Wordsworth), 'ought not to be taken by anyone with weak nerves,' as the top, in many places, scarcely affords room to plant the foot, and is beset with awful precipices on either side. The place, he adds, derives a melancholy interest from the fate of a young man, a stranger, who perished in the Spring of 1805, by falling down the rocks in his attempt to cross over from Wythburn to Patterdale. His remains were not discovered, as we learn from an introduction to a poem by Sir Walter Scott, until three months afterwards, when they were found guarded by a faithful terrier dog, his constant attendant during frequent solitary rambles through the wilds of Westmorland and Cumberland. It appears, from the same note, that the stranger, whose name was Gough, was a young gentleman of talent, and of a most amiable disposition. Both Sir Walter Scott and Mr. Wordsworth have written poems upon the subject. The following is Wordsworth's "Fidelity."

> " A barking sound the shepherd hears,
> A cry, as of a dog or fox ;
> He halts, and searches with his eyes
> Among the scattered rocks.
> And now at distance can discern
> A stirring in a brake of fern,
> And instantly a dog is seen
> Glancing through that covert green.
>
> The dog is not of mountain breed,
> Its motions, too, are wild and shy ;
> With something, as the shepherd thinks,
> Unusual in its cry :
> Nor is there any one in sight
> All round, in hollow or on height ;
> Nor shout, nor whistle strikes his ear,—
> What is the creature doing here ?
>
> It was a cove—a huge recess,
> That keeps till June December's snow
> A lofty precipice in front,
> A silent tarn below !
> Far in the bosom of Helvellyn,
> Remote from public road or dwelling,
> Pathway, or cultivated land ;
> From trace of human foot or hand.
>
> There sometimes doth a leaping fish
> Send through the tarn a lonely cheer,
> The crags repeat the raven's croak,
> In symphony austere :

Thither the rainbow comes—the cloud—
And mists that spread the flying shroud,
And sunbeams, and the sounding blast,
That, if it could, would hurry past,
But that enormous barrier binds it fast.

Not free from boding thoughts, awhile
The shepherd stood; then makes his way
Towards the dog, o'er rocks and stones,
As quickly as he may;
Nor far had gone before he found
A human skeleton on the ground;
The appall'd discoverer with a sigh
Looks round, to learn the history.

From these abrupt and perilous rocks
The man had fallen, that place of fear!
At length upon the shepherd's mind
It breaks, and all is clear:
He instantly recalled the name,
And who he was, and whence he came;
Remember'd, too, the very day,
On which the traveller pass'd this way.

But hear a wonder for whose sake
This lamentable tale I tell,
A lasting monument of words
This wonder merits well.
The dog, which still was hovering nigh,
Repeating the same timid cry,
This dog had been through three months' space,
A dweller in that savage place.

Yes, proof was plain, that since the day
On which the traveller thus had died
The dog had watched about the spot,
Or by his master's side.
How nourished here through such long time
He knows, who gave that love sublime,
And gave that strength of feeling, great
Above all human estimate."

 The summit of Helvellyn is a smooth mossy plain, inclining slightly to the west, and terminating abruptly by broken precipices on the east. On the mountain are two cairns, or piles of stone, called "men," about a quarter of a mile apart, and from an angle in the hill between them the best view of the country northward is to be obtained. The majestic Skiddaw, with Blencathra or Saddleback, on its right, are the most prominent features of the landscape.

THE LEGEND OF BISHOP BLAIZE.

There is an inn at Kendal known by the name of "Bishop Blaize." This Bishop was the patron saint of the wool-combers in England, and the supposed inventor of their art. In *Hone's Year Book* there is an account of two festivals that were formerly held in his honour at Potton, in Bedfordshire, also famous for its wool trade in times gone by. It appears that similar festivals were common to most manufacturing towns, till the early part of last century, and to Kendal among the rest. In the "Book," under the date of Feb. 3rd, a still more particular account of the Saint is given, together with a detail of the ceremonies observed on the Septennial commemoration of his name at Bradford, in Yorkshire, so lately as 1825. Besides being the true patron of wool-combing, the Saint, who died in the fourth century, was famous for curing sore throats. He lived in a cave, and was "very often visited," says the Golden Legend, "by wild beasts whenever a bone stuck in their throats. If it happened that they came while he was at prayer they did not interrupt him, but waiting until he had ended, and never departed without his benediction," A most exemplary man was the Bishop—so exemplary and so holy that Father Ribadaneira relates of him, that when he was scourged by his persecutors "seven holy women anointed themselves with his blood." This having drawn upon them both attention and vengeance, their flesh—out of cruel compliment to the wool-comber, it is to be supposed— was "combed with iron combs"—but strange to say "their wounds ran milk—their flesh became whiter than snow, and angels came visibly and healed their wounds as fast as they were made." They were then, as a last resource, put into the fire. It would not, however, consume them—and this trying the patience of their persecutors to the utmost extreme, they were ordered to be beheaded—and beheaded they were accordingly. St. Blaize was ordered to be drowned in the lake; but he very coolly walked on the water—sat down on it, and invited his tormentors to meet him in the middle. Seventy of them tried to do it, and were drowned; and the Saint having seen them sink, no doubt with great satisfaction, walked to the land very composedly and devoutly, and was then and there beheaded without more ado.

A MOURNFUL LEGEND OF ARA FORCE.

Ara Force rises in the great Dod mountain, part of which forms Gowbarrow Park, one of the most beautiful falls throughout the Lake district. It stands in the Lyulph Tower Garden, an ivy-covered little castle, built for a shooting box by the late Duke of Norfolk; but it is reared on the site of a real old tower, named, it is said, after Ulf, or L'Ulf, the first baron of Greystoke, who gave its name to the lake. The part which surrounds it, and stretches down to the lake, is studded with ancient trees; and the sides of its water-courses, and the depths of its ravine, are luxuriantly wooded. Vast hills, with climbing tracks, rise behind, on which herds of deer are occasionally seen, like brown shadows from the clouds. They are safe there from being startled (as they are in the glades of the park) by strangers who come to find Ara Force by following the sound of the fall. As he sits in the cool damp nook at the bottom of the chasm, where the echo of dashing and gurgling water never dies, and the ferns, long grasses, and ash sprays, wave and quiver everlastingly in the pulsing air; and as, looking up, he sees the slender line of bridge spanning the upper fall he ought to know of the mournful legend which belongs to this place, which Wordsworth has immortalised in his poem of "The Somnambulist." The pathetic legend is thus related:—

The beautiful Emma of Wordsworth's poem was betrothed to Sir Eglamour, a knight who courted her in her father's old tower, and who endeavoured to achieve the hand of his lady-love by performing daring deeds in knight-errantry. The glory he won, poor Emma rejoiced to hear from time to time; these news at length, however, brought bad tidings of his deeds of gallantry in behalf of other distressed ladies, and doubts of his fidelity gradually crept into Emma's devoted heart, disturbed, and caused her weakened mind to travel, and she began to walk in her dreams. Of an evening, in her dream wanderings, she directed her steps towards the holly-tree by the waterfall, where she and her lover had plighted their troth, and safely traversed the dangerous paths, this was the limit of her dream walks. Sir Eglamour, at length, returned in the dead of the night to claim his affianced bride. He wandered towards the trysting-tree, there to rest until the morning should permit him to knock at the gate of her father's tower; but, as he approached the spot he saw a figure in white gliding on before him among the trees. The fair and delicate hand plucked a few holly-leaves, and then let them fall gently into the stream below, with an agonizing sigh upheaving that delicate frame. He stood aghast—outstretched his trembling hand and again withdrew it.—Was it the ghost of his Emma? or was it herself? She stood in a dangerous position; he put out his hand to uphold her: the touch awakened her. In her terror and confusion she fell from his grasp into the torrent, and was carried down the ravine. He followed and rescued her, but she died upon the bank; not, however, with-

I

out having understood that her lover was true, and had come to claim her.

The knight devoted the rest of his days to mourn her; he built himself a cell upon the spot, and became a hermit for her sake.

> "Soul shattered was the knight, nor knew
>   If Emma's ghost it were;
> A boding shade, or if the maid
>   Her very self stood there.
> He touched—What followed who can tell;
>   The soft touch snapped the thread
> Of slumber; shrieking, back she fell,
>   And the stream whirled her down the dell
> Along its foaming bed."

The following lines are from Wordsworth's "Somnambulist"—

> "List ye who pass by Lyulph's Tower
>   At eve; how softly then
> Doth Ara Force, that torrent hoarse,
>   Speak from the woody glen!
> Fit music for a solemn vale!
>   And holier seems the ground,
> To him who catches on the gale
>   The spirit of a mournful tale.
>
> *   *   *   *   *
>
> Wild stream of Ara, hold thy course,
>   Nor fear memorial lays,
> Where clouds that spread in solemn shade
>   Are edged with golden rays!
> Dear art thou to the light of heaven,
>   Though minister of sorrow,
> Sweet is thy voice at pensive even,
>   And thou in lovers' hearts,
> Shalt take thy place with Yarrow."

THE CELEBRATION OF RUSH-BEARING AT GRASMERE CHURCH.

The church of Grasmere is dedicated to St. Oswald, and has been very celebrated, not only for the beauty of its position, and its neighbourhood, but for the annual celebration of rush-bearing. St. Oswald's Day is on the Sunday nearest to the first of August, and the rush-bearing annually takes place at Grasmere on the last Saturday but one in July, and at Ambleside on the following Saturday. Anciently, when the floor of the churches in England were neither paved nor boarded, rushes were indispensable articles of comfort to church-going people; but with the progress of elegance in architecture it became rare to find unpaved churches, and the ceremony of strewing the rushes fell, consequently, into disuse. We find in *Hone's Year Book*, 1831, that the sweet scented flag, or *acorus calamus*, was commonly made use of on these occasions, having been selected originally in consequence of their roots giving out, when bruised by the heat of feet, a very powerful and fragrant odour, resembling that of the myrtle. This plant, however, from its great demand in breweries, under the name of *quassia*, has not been obtainable for many years, and the yellow water iris has been substituted in its place. The rush-bearing at Grasmere generally takes place in the evening, when the children of the village, chiefly girls, parade through the streets to the church, preceded by a band of music, bearing garlands of wild flowers as well as bundles of rushes; the latter of which they deposit on the altar, or strew about the floor of the church. The same annual ceremony was also observed at Ambleside and other places.

THE LAMENT OF THE BORDER WIDOW.

AN AFFECTING BALLAD OF THE BORDER CITY.

Carlisle, the Border City—the city of King Arthur and his knights—is very rich in legendary ballads. The following is founded upon the story of Cockburn of Henderland, a noted disturber of the English districts; who did not, however, suffer at Carlisle, though he had ravaged its neighbourhood; nor at the hands of the English, whose laws he had violated. James the Fifth, scandalised at the excesses of these border reivers, made an excursion into their country in 1529, and executed summary justice upon several of the most turbulent, among others Cockburn of Henderland. He was hanged, by the King's order, over the gate of his own keep or tower, whilst his lady fled to the banks of a mountain stream, called the Henderland Burn, and sat down at the foot of a foaming cataract, to drown, amid the sound of the roaring waters, the noise of the drums that announced the close of her husband's existence. The place where she sat is still shown to the stranger. "The author of the ballad," says Charles Mackay, himself a poet of high merit, "is unknown." It was taken down in the Ettrick Forest, and is as affecting a ballad as any in the language, abounding with touches of genuine pathos, and most lovely simplicity of sorrow. Exquisite is the whole composition, and some of the passages are worthy of the greatest poets:—

> " My love, he built me a bonnie tower,
> And clad it a' wi' lilye flower,
> A brawer bower ye ne'er did see,
> Than my true love he built for me.
>
> There came a man, by middle day
> He spied his sport, and went away,
> And brought the King that very night,
> Who brake my bower, and slew my knight.
>
> He slew my knight to me sae dear,
> He slew my knight and poined his gear,
> My servants all for life did flee
> And left me in extremitie.
>
> I sewed his sheet, making my moan,
> I watched the corpse, myself alone,
> I watched the body night and day,
> No living creature came that way.

I took his body on my back,
And whiles I gaed, and whiles I sat,
I digged a grave and laid him in,
And happed him with the sod sae green.

But think nae ye my heart was sair,
When I laid the mould on his yellow hair!
Oh think nae ye my heart was wae
When I turned about away to gae.

Nae living man I'll love again,
Since that my lovely knight is slain,
Wi' ae lock of his yellow hair
I'll bind my heart for evermair."

A ROMANTIC TRADITION OF EGREMONT CASTLE.

Egremont, in the Ennerdale district of the Lakes, is a little town which looks very pretty from the uplands, and cheerful, too, in spite of its Roman name ("The Mount of Sorrow.") It is distinguished by romantic traditions. It was at the gateway of Egremont Castle that the horn was hung, in crusading days, which was twice blown by the gallant Eustace de Lacy. As the Cumbrians tell: Sir Eustace and his brother Hubert rode forth together to the Holy Wars; and Sir Eustace blew the horn, saying to his brother, "If I fall in Palestine, do thou return and blow the horn, and take possession, that Egremont may not be without a Lacy for its Lord." In Palestine ambition of this Lordship so took possession of Hubert, that he hired ruffians to drown his brother in the Jordan; and the ruffians assured him that the deed was done. He returned home, and stole into the castle by night, not daring to sound the horn. But he soon plucked up spirit, and drowned his remorse in revels. In the midst of a banquet one day, the horn was heard sounding such a blast that the echoes came back from the fells after starting the red deer from his covert, and the wild boar from his drinking at the river.

Hubert knew that none but Eustace could, or would, sound the horn; and he fled by a postern while his brother, Eustace, entered by the gates. Long after, the wretched Hubert came to ask forgiveness from his brother; and having obtained it, retired to a convent, where he practised penance till he died. The ruins of the castle stands on an eminence to the west of the town.

THE SIEGE OF CARLISLE BY "BONNIE PRINCE CHARLIE."

The following account (from the *Gentleman's Magazine*, 1745) derives its interest as being written by an eye witness:—

"On Saturday, the 9th, afternoon, about three o'clock, a body of the rebels appeared at Stanwix Bank, within a quarter of a mile of Carlisle, and it being the market-day there they mixed with the country people returning home, so that it was not possible for the garrison to fire upon them for some time, without risque of injuring their neighbours along with their enemies; but in less than half-an-hour the country people dispersed themselves, and then the garrison of the castle fired a ten-gun battery upon them, which, 'tis believed, killed several; then, night coming on, they retreated to a greater distance from the city, and the garrison stood all night under arms. At two in the morning a thick fog came on, which remained till twelve next day, when it cleared up for about a hour, and then the garrison discovered the rebels approaching to attack the city in three several parties, viz., one at Stanwix Bank, commanded by the Duke of Perth, a second at *Shading Gate Lane*, commanded by the Marquis of Tallibardine, who also had the artillery, and a third in Blackwell Fields, where the Pretender commanded the rest of their body, facing the English Gate.

"Upon discovering these three parties approaching so near the city the garrison fired upon them, viz., the four-gun battery upon the Marquis of Tallibardine, who was heard to say 'Gentlemen, we have not metal for them, retreat;' which they immediately did, and disappeared. The turret guns and the citadel guns were fired upon the Pretender's division, where the white flag was displayed, which was seen to fall; about the same time the nine-gun battery was fired upon the Duke of Perth's division, who also retired. Then the thick fog struck in again, and all the inhabitants of the city expected nothing but a general assault would be made by the rebels, against which the walls were lined with men, and Sir John Pennington, Dr. Waugh, Chancellor; Humphrey Senhouse, Joseph Dacre Dalston, of Acorn Bank, Esqrs., with several other gentlemen of note, stood all night under arms to encourage and assist them. The militia was also drawn up at the foot of Castle Street, to be ready, in case of a forcible attack, to relieve and reinforce the men on the walls. On Monday morning, the fog still continuing thick, the garrison could not observe the situation of the rebels, but heard their pipers playing not far from the English Gate. About ten o'clock a man was let down from the city walls to reconnoitre the enemy, and he found they were retiring towards Warwick Bridge. After noon other spies were likewise detach'd to observe their motions, and discover'd a great number remain'd about Warwick Bridge; but the Pretender, with his guard and attendants, were advanc'd to Brampton, where they lodg'd themselves that night; and on Tuesday they lay idle from all action, except feats of rapine and plunder; for they spent the day in hunting and destroying the sheep of Lord Carlisle's tenants, and bearing off the country people's geese and other poultry. They also seized upon all the horses they could lay hands on, without any question relating to value or property; notwithstanding they declare the design of their expedition is to redress grievances and correct abuses. Tuesday night the rebels slept quietly with full bellies. On Wednesday morning, about ten o'clock, they displayed the white flag at Warwick Bridge end, to which they were about three hours in repairing. About one o'clock, the young Pretender, attended by Lord George Murray, the Duke of Perth, and several others, besides those called his guards, came to them; upon which they formed themselves, and began to march again to Carlisle in the following order:—First, two (named hussars) in Highland dresses, and high rough red caps, like pioneers; next followed half-a-dozen of the chief leaders, followed by a kettle drum; then the Pretender's son, at the head of about one hundred and ten horse, called his guards, two and two a-breast; after these a confused multitude of all sorts of mean people, to the number (as was supposed) of about 6,000. In this order they advanced to the heights of Warwick Moor, when they halted about half-a-hour, and took an attentive view of the city. From thence the foot took the lead, and so marched to Carlisle about three in the afternoon, when they began a fresh assault, and the citizens renewed their fire. On Thursday, it was discovered that the rebels had thrown up a trench, which intimidated the town, and in a consultation it was resolved to capitulate; a deputation was sent to the Pretender at Brampton, and the town and castle delivered up on Friday morning."

The victory of the Stuart party was but of short duration and little benefit. The Duke of Cumberland arrived with his army on Saturday, the 21st of December, the garrison displayed a flag of truce, and surrendered. Gallows Hill, about a mile south of Carlisle, was the place of execution selected for the unfortunate Scotchmen. Until nearly the end of the last century the remains of the gibbet were to be seen here; and at the foot of it, the ashes of the fire used in burning the bodies of those who suffered for high treason.

With this event ends the historical interest of Carlisle. The walls of the city long displayed the hideous mementos of the downfall of the Stuarts—a circumstance alluded to by David Hume, in his inscription on the windows of the Bush Inn, when he visited Carlisle two or three years afterwards:—

"Here chiks in eggs for breakfast sprawls;
Here Godless boys, God's glory squall.
While Scotchmen's heads adorn the wall,
But CORBY'S WALKS atone for all."

Sir Walter Scott imagined these to be the only verses Hume ever wrote. In a letter to Mr. Morritt, dated Abbotsford, 2nd October, 1815, and published in Lockhart's Life, Sir Walter facetiously says, in allusion to these four lines, "Would it not be a good quiz to advertise 'The poetical works of David Hume,' with notes, critical, historical, and so forth, with a historical inquiry into the use of eggs for breakfast, a physical discussion on the causes of their being addled; a history of the English Church music, and of the choir at Carlisle in particular; a full account of the affairs of 1745, with the trials, last speeches, and so forth of the poor *plaids*, who were strapped up at Carlisle; and lastly, a full and particular description of Corby, with the genealogy of every family who ever possessed it? I think, even without more than the usual waste of margin, the poems of David would make a decent twelve shilling touch."

THE POET SHELLEY'S RESIDENCE AT THE LAKES.

Mr. De Quincey informs us of some circumstances connected with Shelley's residence at Keswick, near the famous Druid's Circle.

"Between two and three years after Shelley's expulsion from Oxford," says Mr. De Quincey, "he married a beautiful girl, named Westbrook. She was respectably connected; but had not moved in a rank corresponding to Shelley's; and that accident brought him into my own neighbourhood, for his family, already estranged from him, were now thoroughly irritated by what they regarded as a *mésalliance*, and withdrew, or greatly reduced, his pecuniary allowances. Such, at least, was the story current. In this embarassment his wife's father made over to him an annual income of £200, and, as economy had become important, the youthful pair—both, in fact, still children—came down to the lakes, supposing this region of Cumberland and Westmorland to be a sequestered place, which it *was*, for eight months in the year; and also to be a cheap place—which it was *not*. Another motive to this choice arose from the then Duke of Norfolk. He was an old friend of Shelley's family, and generously refused to hear a word of the young man's errors, except where he could do anything to relieve him from the consequences. His Grace possessed the beautiful estate of Gowbarrow Park, on Ullswater, and other estates of greater extent in the same two counties; his own agents he had directed to furnish any accommodation that might meet Shelley's views; and he had written to some gentlemen amongst his agricultural friends in Cumberland, requesting them to pay such neighbourly attentions to the solitary young people as circumstances might place in their power. This bias being impressed upon Shelley's wanderings, naturally brought him to Keswick, as the most central and the largest of the little towns dispersed amongst the lakes. Southey, made aware of the interest taken in Shelley by the Duke of Norfolk, with his usual kindness, immediately called upon him; and the ladies of Southey's family subsequently made an early call upon Mrs. Shelley. One of them mentioned to me, as occurring in this first visit, an amusing expression of the youthful matron, which, four years later, when I heard of her gloomy end, recalled with the force of a pathetic contrast, that icy arrest then chaining up her youthful feet for ever. The Shelley's had been induced by one of their new friends, Mr. Calvert, to take part of a house standing about a mile out of Keswick, on the Penrith Road; more, I believe, in that friend's intention, for the sake of bringing them easily within his hospitalities, than for any beauty in the place. And whilst walking in this, one of the Southey party asked Mrs. Shelley if the garden had been let with *their* part of the house. 'Oh, no,' she replied, 'the garden is not ours; but then, you know, the people let us run about in it whenever Percy and I are tired of sitting in the house.' The *naïveté* of this expression, 'run about, contrasting so picturesquely with the intermitting efforts of the girlish wife at supporting a matronlike gravity now that she was doing the honours of her house to married ladies, caused all the party to smile. And *me* it caused profoundly to sigh, four years later, when the gloomy death of this young creature, now frozen in a distant grave, threw back my remembrance upon her fawn-like playfulness, which, unconsciously to herself, the girlish phrase of *run about* so naturally betrayed.

"At that time," continues Mr. De Quincey, "I had a cottage myself in Grasmere, just thirteen miles distant from Shelley's new abode. As he had then written nothing of any interest, I had no motive for calling upon him, except by way of showing any little attentions in my power to a brother Oxonian, and to a man of letters. Some neighbourly advantages I might certainly have placed at Shelley's disposal—Grasmere, for instance, itself, which tempted at that time by a beauty that had not been sullied; Wordsworth, who then lived at Grasmere; and Professor Wilson at

Elleray, nine miles further; finally, my own library, which, being rich in the wickedest of German speculations, would naturally have been more to Shelley's taste than the Spanish library of Southey.

But all these temptations were negatived for Shelley by his sudden departure. Off he went in a hurry; but *why* he went, or *whither* he went, I did not inquire; not guessing the interest which he would create in my mind six years later, by his 'Revolt of Islam.' A Life of Shelley, in a Continental edition of his works says, that he went to Edinburgh and to Ireland. Some time after, we at the Lakes, heard that he was living in Wales. But events were hurrying upon his heart of hearts. Within less than ten years the whole career of his life was destined to revolt. Within that space he had the whole burden of life and death to exhaust; he had all his suffering to suffer, and all his work to work."

REGATTA ON DERWENTWATER.—1782.

Bassenthwaite-water was the *first* lake that was honoured with one of those amusements called Regattas; this was on the 24th of August, 1780. Another was exhibited on the 1st of August, 1781 (when the *swimming sweepstakes* were introduced); and the last on the 4th September, 1782. This species of entertainment was begun on Derwentwater, on the 28th August, 1781, and has continued, with intermissions, till the present time, 1881.

ROMAN REMAINS.

Upon Hutton Moor, and on the north side of the great road, could be traced the path of the Roman way that leads from old Penrith, or Plumpton-wall, in a line almost due west to Keswick. Upon the moor are the traces of a large encampment that the road traverses. And a little beyond the eighth mile-post, on the left, at Whitbarrow, are strong vestiges of a square encampment. The Roman road, beyond that, is met with in the enclosed fields of Whitbarrow, and is known by the farmers from the opposition they meet with in ploughing across it. After that it is found entirely on the common called "Greystoke Low Moor." About 1779 a new road was formed on the *agger* of it. In the year 1772, near Little Blencow, in removing a heap of stones, two urns were taken up, about 2½-ft. high, made of very coarse earth, and crusted on both sides with a brown clay, the tops remarkably wide, and covered with a red flat stone. Besides ashes and bones, each urn had a small cup within it, of a fine clay, in the shape of a tea-cup. One was pierced in the centre of the bottom part. The place where they were taken up is called "Lodden-how," within twenty yards of the road between Penrith and Skelton, and about 200 yards from the Roman road. Also on the banks of the Peteril, a curious altar was found about 1779. It was three feet four inches in height, and nearly sixteen inches square. It had been thrown down from the upper ground, and the corners broken off in the fall. The front had been filled with an inscription; the letters short and square, but not one word remains legible. On the right-hand side is the *patera*, with a handle, and underneath the *secespita*. On the opposite side is the Ampula, and from its lip a serpent or viper descends in waves. The back part is rude, as if intended to stand against a wall. The emblems are in excellent preservation. That the Romans have had engagements at Kirkstone-pass is evident, from the Roman arms that were found (1779) in the adjoining moss, and the many heaps of stones collected thereabouts, which have the appearance of barriers.

REMAINS OF PAINTED GLASS IN BOWNESS CHURCH.

In Bowness there is nothing so remarkable as some remains of painted glass, in the east window of the church, whose low, square tower and weather-worn look, lifts up its old broad-faced clock, the hands of which seem treading the footsteps of time, as they have done for centuries, while its old appearance wears a grey, venerable look that harmonizes well with all around. The churchyard holds the remains of Richard Watson, Bishop of Llandaff, who lived and died at Calgarth House, on the margin of the lake, July 1st, 1816, aged 79. The ancient and elaborately-painted chancel window was brought from Furness Abbey, and is thus described in "Hutchinson's Excursions":—

"The present remains of this window show that it has contained very fine colouring in its former state. The arms of France and England quartered, are well preserved at the top of the window. The design is a crucifixion in figures as large as life. By the hands, feet and parts remaining, it seems to have been of singular beauty. On the dexter side of the crucifixion is St. George slaying the dragon: on the sinister, the Virgin Mary;—an uncouth assemblage. Beneath, are the figures of a knight and his lady kneeling; before whom are a group of kneeling monks, over whose heads is written: W. Hartley, Tho. Honton, and other names, by the breaking of the glass rendered not legible." The glass is a fine specimen of ancient art, and consists of thousands of fragments joined together—

All diamonded with panes of quaint device,
And twilight saints, and dim emblazonings.
And shielded 'scutcheons blush'd with blood of kings and queens.

Bowness Church is a picturesque time-worn building, beautifully begirt by its ancient trees, and its quiet

"God's Acre," where every grave stone is lapped in posied plots and bright little interspaces of well-kept green, with here and there an overhanging bough; and it is a delightful thing to sit upon a bench outside, when clouds of midges are whirling in the glow of a declining day, and swallows are flitting around the old tower, and the gloaming begins to bend with the solemn colouring of the night, whilst the sounds of sacred evensong float from the open doors into the resting village.

OPTICAL ILLUSIONS.

Towards the south-east corner of Whernside, some singular properties may be observed in the black earth which composes the soil in the higher parts of the vale, in various mossy places. It is a kind of putrified earth, which, in the night, resembles fire, when it is agitated by being trod upon. The effects it produces in a dark evening is truly curious and amusing. Strangers are always surprised and often frightened, to see their own and horses' legs besprinkled to all appearance with fire, and sparks of it flying in every direction, as if struck out of the ground from under their feet. They are as much alarmed with it, as the country people are with the Will-o'-the-wisp. Though the dark and dreary moor is broken into thousands of luminous particles, like so many glow-worms, when troubled by the benighted traveller, yet if any of this natural phosphorus is brought before a lighted candle, its splendour immediately vanishes, and it shrinks back into its original dull and dark state of sordid dirt.

Another optical illusion are the Castle Rocks of St. John's. The vale of St. John's is a very narrow dell, hemmed in by mountains, through which a small brook makes many meanderings, washing little enclosures of grass ground, which stretch up the risings of the hills.

In the widest part of the dale the beholder is struck with the appearance of an ancient ruined castle, which seems to stand upon the summit of a little mount, the mountains around forming an amphitheatre. This massive bulwark shows a front of various towers, and makes an awful, rudely, and gothic appearance, with its lofty turrets and rugged battlements,—bending arches, buttresses, and galleries may be traced; the greatest antiquity stands characterized in its architecture.

Curiosity is aroused, and the traveller prepares to make a nearer approach; when that curiosity is put upon the rack, by his being assured, that if he advances, certain *genii*, who govern the place, by virtue of their supernatural arts and necromancy, will strip it of all its beauties, and by enchantment transform the magic walls. The vale, too, seems well adapted for the habitation of such beings; its gloomy recesses and retirements look like haunts of evil spirits; there was no delusion in the report, and the visitor is soon convinced of its truth, for this piece of antiquity, so venerable and noble in its aspect, as he draws near, changes its figure and proves no other than a shaken massive pile of rocks, which stand in the midst of this little vale, disunited from the adjoining mountains, and have so much the real form and resemblance of a castle that they bear the name of the CASTLE ROCKS OF ST. JOHN'S. The delusion is a source of much laughter and merriment when it is discovered.

GRAPHIC DESCRIPTION OF A STAG HUNT IN 1773.

From Hutchinson's "An Excursion to the Lakes," we quote the following vivid description of a stag chase:—" Mr. Hazel, of Delmain, is possessed of the Chase of Martindale, which borders on the lake (Ullswater), and includes most of the heights which lie upon the eastern side. The lands of his manor being of customary tenure, are attended with this badge of servility: the tenants are bound to attend their lord's hunt within this chase once a year, which is called in their court role a *Boon Hunt.* On this occasion they have each their district allotted on the boundaries of the chase, where they are stationed, to prevent the stag flying beyond the liberty. A stag chase was promised the gentlemen of the county on the marriage of William Hazel, Esq., heir apparent of the house of Delmain, whose excellent character and merit had rendered the occasion a cause of great festivity in the neighbourhood; but as I was not fortunate enough to be present at this diversion," continues Mr. Hutchinson, "shall beg the reader's attention to a description given me by one who had enjoyed a similar scene:—

"'A stag having been selected from his herd, the hounds were conducted to the copse, where he lay inattentive to the dangers which surrounded him. On being roused, he stretched his limbs, advanced his antlers with solemn dignity, and looked disdainfully upon the approaching hunters. He quitted the cover, and in contempt of the threatenings of his foes, seemed scarce to touch the ground, as he bounded upon his springing pasterns and made his flight in vaultings and sportive leaps. The cry of the hounds was singularly melodious, being re-echoed from shore to shore, added to the music of the horns. The hills were cloathed with spectators;—on the lake were several barges with colours displayed, and other boats, crowded with people. The stag at first took the heights, where sometimes he was seen climbing the mountains with incredible swiftness, whilst the hounds appeared in a slower train, pursuing, yet losing ground, so much did he seem to outstrip them. At other times the interposing mountains robbed us of the sight, but indulged us with the music of the cry, from the melody of which, attention was not diverted by having the pack in view. Again they came in sight—

the stag flew over every fence as an arrow from the bow—the hounds appeared to gain ground; the various windings of the fugitive along the steeps were all in view. At length he found his flight and speed did not avail him; he meditated to save himself by artifice, submitting to descend into the lower grounds, and quit the hills. The people who attended, perceiving the well-known signal of his declining speed, with their shouts from every quarter, made each vale and cliff resound. Echo deceived our ears in a surprising manner, for the shouts were so repeated, as if the whole extensive circus was crowded with people, and the huzza given by tens of thousands. Instantly all the vessels on the lake were put in motion, and the oars were busied in flying to that quarter to which the stag advanced. It is their usual custom, when pressed by the hounds, to take the water—to plunge into the lake, and trust to their swimming. Many of the pack jumped into the water—and the chase was continued even in the lake. The unhappy stag found, though he escaped his common enemy, yet other foes, which rendered all his efforts for safety vain. The boats enclosed him, and brought him again to shore. To prolong the diversion, his distress was doubled; a respite was given for some moments;—hope arose upon his heart, but of short existence! With looks of terror he soon beheld his pursuers upon him. After many flights and once more watering, the noble fugitive was driven to his forlorn hope;—his timid nature was changed by necessity, and courage arose from despair;—he stood, and with his horns bayed the approaching hounds—his last and sad ineffectual efforts. He was seized, and by the hunters saved from being torn piecemeal by the dogs.'"

To this despicably cruel scene Mr. Hutchinson adds the following well-timed reflections.—

"Compassion and the finer feelings have nothing to do with the chase:—were man to give way to the sympathetic sentiments the distress and misery of the innocent animal which is pursued and hunted down, would overcome the melody of the cry, and the beauty of those artifices which the pursued employs in vain to save his life.—Let such men avoid the chase. Men of robust and hardy constitutions feel the least compassion or sentiment, and trust the least to thought. Such are the heroes of the hunt. I have been told, that after the captive has received his death's wound from the keeper, it is usual for the hunters to compleat their joy, by staining each other's face with the gore."

"PUNCH" AND THE POET LAUREATE (WORDSWORTH),
OR A DIFFERENCE OF OPINION ON THE PROJECTED WINDERMERE RAILWAY (1844).

The Laureate, in one of his latest sonnets, pours out his "vial of wrath" on the profane idea of introducing railways through the sublime country in which he had made his home. It was a selfish effusion, we must admit; but something extenuating might be said for the poet, for had he not lived here for half a century in that peace and solitude which he loved so well, and which influenced his gifted mind to pour out immortal verse? The sonnet runs thus:—

> "Is there no nook of English ground secure
>   From rash assault? Schemes of retirement sown
> In youth, and 'mid the busy world kept pure
>   As when their earliest flowers of hope were blown,
> Must perish. How can they this blight endure?
>   And must he, too, his old delights disown,
> Who, scorns a false utilitarian lure,
>   'Mid his paternal fields at random thrown?
> Baffle the threat, bright scene, from Orrest Head,
>   Given to the pausing traveller's rapturous glance!
> Plead for thy peace thou beautiful romance
> Of Nature! And if human hearts be dead—
>   Speak, passing winds:—ye torrents with pure, strong,
> And constant voice, protest against the wrong."

To this sonnet, Mr. Wordsworth pleads, in a note, that this may not be considered a mere poetical effusion, but as his calm and settled opinion upon the proposed railway, and the introduction of steam into such a remote locality.

"Punch," a few weeks after the appearance of Mr. Wordsworth's sonnet, also gave to the world his views of the introduction of steam into this locality, which we insert that the reader may have the opportunity of comparing the one with the other. It is entitled—

"BY THE LAUREATE."

"What incubus, my goodness! have we here,
Cumbering the bosom of our lovely lake?
A steamboat, as I live!—without mistake!—
Puffing and splashing over Windermere!
What inharmonious shouts assail mine ear?
Shocking poor Echo, that perforce replies—
'Ease her!' and 'Stop her!'—frightful and horrid cries,
Mingling with frequent pop of ginger beer.
Hence, ye profane!—To Greenwich or Blackwall
From London Bridge—go! steam it if ye will,
Ye Cockneys! and of Whitebait eat your fill;
But this is not the place for you at all!
I almost think that, if I had my will,
I'd sink your vessel with a cannon ball!"

The poetical history, however, of the Kendal and Windermere Railway will not be complete without the following sonnet, also suggested by Wordsworth's, which appeared shortly afterwards from the pen of Mr. Moncton Milnes, since created Lord Houghton:—

"The hour may come—nay, must,—in these our days
  When the harsh steam-car with the cataract's shout,
  Shall mingle its swift roll, and motley rout
Of multitudes these mountain echoes raise.
And *thou*, the patriarch of these pleasant ways,
  Canst hardly grudge that crowded streets send out,
  In Sabbath glee, the sons of care and doubt,
To read these scenes by light of thine own lays.
Disordered laughter and encounter rude,
  The poet's finer sense perchance may pain;

Yet many a glade and nook of solitude
For quiet walk and thought will still remain,
Where he the poor intruders may elude,
Nor lose one golden dream for all their homely gain."

THE ENGRAVER OF THE ROCKS.

Under this heading we find in Charles Mackay's "English Lakes," that whilst having a row on lake Windermere, his boatman told him that at a short distance on the eastern side of the lake, were some inscriptions on the rocks, which were the greatest curiosities of the place. The "Guide-book" having made no mention of them, we were the more anxious to see what they were, and were rowed ashore accordingly, at a point not far from Lowwood Inn. Here we found every smooth surface afforded by the rocks—every slab on the stratified formation—covered with inscriptions, engraved with much toil, in letters varying from six to twenty-four inches in height. On one large red stone, of at least ten feet square, was engraved — ' 1833. — MONEY, LIBERTY, WEALTH, PEACE ';—a catalogue of blessings very much to be desired. On another stone was the simple date, ' 1688 ': expressive enough of the engraver's political sentiments. And on another, in larger characters, ' A SLAVE LANDING ON THE BRITISH STRAND, BECOMES FREE.' All the largest stones and slabs, some of which were horizontal, others vertical, and the rest inclined at various angles, and the whole of them giving evidence that the place had formerly been a quarry—were covered with inscriptions of a like purport. The following are a few of the most striking. One immense surface of rock bore the following names, which are transcribed in the original order. — ' SUN, BULWER, DRYDEN, DAVY, BURNS, SCOTT, BURDETT, GARRICK, KEMBLE, GRAY, KEAN, MILTON, HENRY BROUGHAM, JAMES WATT, PROFESSOR WILSON, DR. JENNER'; to which were added the words, in characters equally conspicuous,—'THE LIBERTY OF THE PRESS.' 'MAGNA CHARTA.' This slab was a testimony apparently, of the engraver's admiration of great intellect. One close alongside of it was of a different style, and bore the date of '1836,' followed by the words, 'WILLIAM IV. PRESIDENT JACKSON. LOUIS PHILIPPE. BRITANNIA RULES THE WAVES.' Next to that again was a still larger surface of rock, on which was indented, 'NATIONAL DEBT, £800,000,000.' 'O SAVE MY COUNTRY, HEAVEN!' 'GEORGE III. & WILLIAM PITT.' 'MONEY IS THE SINEW OF WAR.' 'FIELD MARSHAL WELLINGTON.' 'HEROIC ADMIRAL NELSON.' 'CAPTAIN COOK.' 'ADMIRAL RODNEY.' One stone, at least eight feet square, bore but one word in letters a yard long, and that was significant enough, viz.—'STEAM.' On enquiring of the boatman, who it was that had expended so much labour, he pointed out another stone, on which were the words, 'JOHN LONGMIRE, ENGRAVER.' and informed us that it was a person of that name, who had spent about six years of his prime in this work—labouring here alone, and in all weathers—and both by night and by day. He took great pleasure in the task, and was, as the boatman took great pains to impress upon us, rather 'dull' at the time. This phrase, as he afterwards explained, implies, in this part of the country, that he was deranged; and I thought, when looking with renewed interest, upon these mementos of his ingenuity and perseverance, misapplied though they were, that it was a happy circumstance that an afflicted creature could have found solace under calamity, in a manner so harmless. There was a method in the work, and a sense too in the poor man's ideas, which showed that his sympathies were in favour of the moral and intellectual advancement of mankind; and that, amid the last feeble glimmerings of his own reason, he could do honour to those whose intellect had benefited and adorned our age. I could learn no further particulars of him,—our friend, the boatman, not being able to say whether he was dead or alive, or whether his 'dulness' had ever manifested itself in a more disorderly manner than in these inscriptions."

THE ROCKS OF LODORE.

Dr. Dalton in his elegant poem addressed to two young ladies at Whitehaven, speaking of the rocks of Lodore, between which is the cascade made so celebrated by its " rush and its roar " (and appropriately rendered by Southey in his unique description,) flows thence into Lake Derwent, has the following reflections :—

"Horrors like these at first alarm,
But soon with savage grandeur charm,
And raise to noblest thought the mind ;
Thus, nigh thy fall, Lodore reclined,
The craggy cliff, impending wood,
Whose shadows mix o'er half the flood
The gloomy clouds which, solemn fall,
Scarce lifted by the languid gale
O'er the cap'd hill and darkened vale ;
The ravening Kite and bird of Jove,
Which round the ærial ocean rove,
And floating on the billowy sky,
With full expanded pennons fly
Their fluttering or their bleating prey,
Thence with death-dooming eye survey,
Channels by rocky torrents torn,
Rocks to the lakes in thunder borne,
Or such as o'er our heads appear
Suspended in their mid career,
To start again at His command
Who rules fire, water, air and land,
I view with wonder and delight,
A pleasing, though an awful sight ;
For seen with them the verdant isles
Soften with more delicious smiles,
More tempting to me their opening bowers,
More lively glow the purple flowers,
More smoothly slopes the border gay
In fairer circle bends the bay,

> And last, to fix our wand'ring eyes,
> Thy roofs, O Keswick, brighter rise,
> The lake and lofty hills between,
> Where giant Skiddaw shuts the scene."

PROFESSOR WILSON AT WASTDALE.

The Author of " Rambles in the Lake Country," in his wanderings in the Lake District, encountered at Wastdale Head, in the person of an innkeeper there, one of the most characteristic specimens that could well be found of a genuine old Laker—William Ritson. " I was most interested," says the writer, "in Ritson's anecdotes of famous men who visited Wastdale. He had wandered many a day with Professor Wilson, Wordsworth, De Quincey and others. Ritson had been a famous wrestler in his youth, and had won many a country belt in Cumberland. He once wrestled with Wilson, and threw him twice out of three falls. But he owned the Professor was 'a varra bad un to lick.' Wilson beat him at jumping. He could jump twelve yards in three jumps, with a great stone in each hand. Ritson could only manage eleven and three quarters. 'T' furst time 'at Professor Wilson cam to Was'dle Head,' said Ritson, ' he hed a tent set up in a field, an' he gat it weel stock'd wi' bread, an' beef, an' cheese, an' rum, an' ale, an' sic like. Then he gedder't up my granfadder, an' Thomas Tyson, an' Isaac Fletcher, an' Joseph Stable, an' aad Robert Grave, an' some mair, an' theer was gay deed amang 'em. Then, nowt wad sarra, but he mun hev a bwoat, an' they mun a' hev a sail. Well, when they gat into t' bwoat, he tell'd 'em to be particklar careful, for he was liable to git giddy in t' head, an' if yan ov his giddy fits sud chance to cum on, he mud happen tummle in t' watter. Well, that pleased 'em all gaily weel, an' they said they'd take varra girt care on him. Then he leaned back an' called oot that they mun pull quicker. So they did, and what does

Wilson du then, but topples ower eb'm ov his back i' t' watter wid a splash. Then theer was a girt cry—
"'Eh, Mr. Wilson's i' 't watter!" an' yan click't, an' anudder click't, but nean o' them cud git hod on him, an' there was sic a scrow as nivver. At last, yan o' them gat him round t' neck as he popped up at teal o' t' bwoat, an Wilson taad him to kep a gud hod, for he mud happen slip him ageàn. But what, it was nowt but yan ov his bits o' pranks, he was smirkin' an' laughin' all t' time. Wilson was a fine, gay, girt-hearted fellow, as strang as a lion, an' as lish as a trout, an' he hed sic' antics as nivver man hed. Whativver ye sed tull him ye'd get your change back for it gaily seun. . . Aa remember, theer was a "murry neet" at Wastd'le Head that varra time, an' Wilson an' t' aad parson was their amang t' rest. When they'd gitten a bit òn, Wilson mead a sang aboot t' parson. He mead it reet off o' t' stick end. He began wi' t' parson furst, then he gat to t' Pope, an' then he turn'd it to th' devil, an' sic like, till he hed 'em fallin' off their cheers wi' fun. T' parson was quite stunn'd, an' rayder vex't an' all, but, at last he burst oot laughin' wi' t' rest. He was like. Naabody could staand it. . . T' sàem neet theer was yan o' their wives cum to fetch her husband heàm, an' she was rayder ower strang i' t' tung wi' him afore t' heàl comp'ny. Well, he tuk it a' i' gud pairt, but as he went away he shouted oot t' aad minister: "'Od dang ye, parson, it wor ye at teed us two togidder! . . It was' a' life an' murth amang us, as lang as Professor Wilson was at Wastd'le Head.'"

DE QUINCEY.

The following brief extract from the life of De Quincey, may be here appropriately placed:

"It was in the year 1807 that De Quincey made the acquaintance of Coleridge, Wordsworth, and

Southey; and on quitting college in 1808 he took up his abode at the Lakes, and became one of the intellectual brotherhood there constituted by these men. Wilson was a resident at the Lakes about the same time. The difference between De Quincey and the Lakists was—that his element was exclusively prose. Like Coleridge, but with peculiarities sufficient to distinguish him from that thinker, he philosophised, and analysed, and speculated in sympathy with the new literary movement of which the Lake party was a manifestation. He resided ten or eleven years at the Lakes; and during these ten or eleven years we are to suppose him increasing his knowledge of Greek, of German, and of Universal History and Literature.

"In point of time De Quincey preceded Carlyle as a literary medium between Germany and this country; and some of his earliest literary efforts were translations from Lessing, Richter, and other German authors.

"These literary efforts, begun while he was still a student at the Lakes, were continued with growing abundance after he left them in 1819."

FOX HOW, THE LAKE RESIDENCE OF DR. ARNOLD.

Fox How was long the residence of the famous Dr. Arnold. The name may seem curious, but it was given the place in ancient times. "How" is a frequent name in the Lake district, it is from O. N. (*haugr*), a sepulchral mound. Sometimes the remains of a warrior have been found in the hills so called, but the word seems to have been applied to any mound-like hill. The home of the Arnold's is a beautiful place in itself, but made more so by the remembrance of the good work that has been done here. Here the *History of Rome* was written. Here also Arnold used to gather around him the young scholars who were children of his nature. Since his death it has remained a hallowed spot for the sons of old Rugby. Dr. Arnold gave the three roads between Rydal and Grasmere their names: the highest, "Old Corruption"; the middle, "Bit-by-bit Reform"; the lowest and most level, "Radical Reform." Wordsworth and his sister Dorothy also added to these new Pilgrim's Progress names, having called a spot "Point Rash Judgment." Along the beautiful walks surrounding Fox How, Arnold and his friends studied, thought, succeeded; and sometimes they would form reading parties in some charming nook among the lakes. "I came to Fox How about three weeks ago to meet Matt," writes Clough from Patterdale, July, 1844, and goes on to describe their ways: "We began with—breakfast, 8; work, 9.30 to 2.30; bathe, dinner, walk, and tea, 2.30 to 9.30; work, 9.30 to 11. We now have revolutionized to the following constitution, as yet hardly advanced beyond paper. Breakfast, 8; work, 9.30 to 1.30; bathe, dinner, 1.30 to 3; work, 3 to 6; walk, *ad infinitum;* tea, ditto. M. has gone out fishing, when he ought properly to be working, it being nearly four o'clock, and to-day proceeding in theory according to Constitution No. 2. It has, however, come on to rain furiously; so Walrond, who is working sedulously at Herodotus, and I who am writing to you, rejoice to think that he will get a good wetting."

The most pathetic incident of modern literary history is the death at forty-three of Arthur Clough, the close friend of Dr. Arnold and Tennyson. Though his body is buried at Florence, his heart is enshrined in the undying love of those who knew him in England and America. In the September of 1861 he was rambling with Tennyson in the Pyrenees —he seeking health, Tennyson revisiting the spots where he had wandered with Arthur Hallam, thirty-one years before. In less than a month from the time they parted, this second of the Arthurs Tennyson loved was dead, and a quotation from "In Memoriam" is inscribed on the Grasmere cenotaph·

> "Now thy brows are cold
> We see thee as thou art and know,
> Thy likeness to the wise below
> Thy kindred with the great of old."

AN ENTERTAINING COACHMAN.

For many years prior to 1866 one John Sheldon drove the coach from Windermere railway station to Keswick, and an entertaining old coachman he was, and full of local information concerning the places the coach was driven through. On one occasion in driving from Patterdale, he remarked: "Now, gentlemen," he would say to his riders, "as you have come all the way from London to see this beautiful scenery, you would, of course, like to know the names of the hills, mountains, knolls, and rivers; we call them 'becks' about here for shortness. Well, gentlemen, that wooded hill on the left hand is Mell Fell, a rare place for bird's nesting, blackberrying, and nutting. The hill behind us is Saddleback, called by some Blencathra. Looking straight along the line of rail you will see Newland Dod, in the beautiful Vale of Newlands, and the hill on the left of it is Catbells, uprising from the shores of the charming Derwentwater. The three round-headed, undulating hills on our left hand is the back of the poetical Helvellyn; you don't see so much of Helvellyn from this side as from the other. I have driven along the Keswick road, under the shadow of Helvellyn, many thousands of times. The mountain begins at Dunmail Raise, above Grasmere, and ends in the poetical Vale of St. John, a distance of seven miles. Sir Walter Scott's poem—

'As I climbed the dark brow of the mighty Helvellyn'—

is familiar to every one; and the Vale of St. John is named in the 'Bridal of Triermain.'

"This is Matterdale Moor we are now crossing. The farmers have the right of grazing so many sheep, according to the size of their farms, by paying the small fee of one shilling annually to the Lord of the Manor. There is fine lichens here and on Helvellyn for the hogs." "Hogs! I don't see any hogs," said an elderly rider, whom John afterwards wormed out was a retired pork butcher who was "doing the tourist." "Well," said John, "not pigs, but you see the small sheep running about? they are a peculiar breed, very hardy, very sweet eating, and are called 'hogs' for the first year, when stripped of their fleece they are called 'twinters,' and when stripped of their second fleece they are called 'thrunters,' so that's pretty near to 'grunters;' but when killed they are called by the butchers 'Helvellyn mutton.'

"You see yonder white farm-house, on the rising ground on the right hand? Looking direct over it you will observe a sharp point in the distance; that is the highest peak of the Helvellyn mountain. We now descend the hill into the village of Dockray, and water the horses at the 'Royal' Hotel. The landlady and I once fell out; so instead of watering the horses at the 'Royal,' I carried a tin can, hooked on to the back of the coach, and stopped at the brook close by, and watered them there. It was not long before she called out—'Father, why don't thee water thy horses here, now?' and we have been good friends ever since. *She found out the loss in bitter beer.* I'm not her father, but they call me 'father' about here."

John wrote some quaint lines about the Ullswater coach, and here they are:—

> "Arriving at Troutbeck, without botheration
> Ask for John Sheldon's coach—'crack whip' at the station.
> Two-and-sixpence, you'll own, is a moderate fare,
> To be driven to Patterdale—'devil-me-care.'

> He'll point out each mountain and beck in the vales
> Of Matterdale, Dockray, Glencoin, Patterdale,
> Describe all the wonders ever heard of or seen,
> And jingle his jokes, too—all right—all serene."

CROSTHWAITE CHURCH AND SOUTHEY'S TOMB.

Thomas Martin, "The Ringer," had great reverence for the name of Southey, and it was most agreeable to meet with an intelligent man who had been familiar with the once Poet Laureate. Martin would say to visitors to the Church, as he uncovered a full-length figure of the poet, "Mr. Southey, in a tour through the Lakes, was so struck with the beauty of Keswick, and the situation of Greta Hall, which was to be let at the time, that he at once decided on taking it as a residence." The figure of the poet is reclining on a couch, beautifully sculptured in Carrara marble, by Mr. Lough, and executed in his best manner, at a cost of £1,100. The baptismal font in this Church is supposed to be 700 years old.

Pointing to a monk's head, painted on the north window, Martin would say, "It is not known how old it is. You see the holy man holds a bell in his hand, ready to ring an alarm-appeal should the devil attempt to enter by the north door; the door-way has been built up, so that there is not much fear. Such was the superstition until Mr. Southey came to live among us, and in the poet's endeavour to remove the feeling, he selected his own grave in the north-west part of the churchyard, as an example to his neighbours; and the result now is that that once-neglected spot in the churchyard is the most favoured and thickly dotted with gravestones." Martin would then conduct his visitors to the top of the Church tower, "where," he said, "Mr. Southey loved to sit on a summer's afternoon, and read." There was a stool on the flat leaden roof, and the "Ringer," placing it in a particular position, he continued, "This is where Mr. Southey loved to sit; he would spend hours here."

In the north-west corner of Crosthwaite Churchyard lies the mortal remains of Robert Southey, beneath a square closed tomb, with the following inscription upon it:—

HERE LIES
THE BODY OF
ROBERT SOUTHEY, LL.D.,
POET LAUREATE.
BORN AUGUST 12, 1774; DIED MARCH 21, 1843.
FORTY YEARS A RESIDENT IN THIS PARISH;
ALSO OF
EDITH, HIS WIFE,
BORN MAY 20, 1774; DIED NOV. 16, 1837.

"I AM THE RESURRECTION AND THE LIFE, SAITH THE LORD."

The following is the inscription on the west end of the monument in the church:—

Sacred
TO THE MEMORY OF
ROBERT SOUTHEY,
WHOSE MORTAL REMAINS ARE INTERRED IN THE ADJOINING CHURCHYARD.
HE WAS BORN AT BRISTOL, AUG. XII. M.DCC.LXXIV.
AND DIED,
AFTER A RESIDENCE OF NEARLY XL. YEARS, AT GRETA HALL, IN THIS PARISH,
MARCH XXI. M.DCCC.XLIII.

THIS MONUMENT WAS ERECTED BY FRIENDS OF ROBERT SOUTHEY.

At the east end of the tomb are the following lines, from the pen of his venerable friend, the late Poet Laureate, Wordsworth :—

Ye Vales and Hills, whose beauty hither drew
The Poet's steps, and fixed him here, on you
His eyes have closed ! And ye, loved Books, no more
Shall Southey feed upon your precious lore,
To Works that ne'er shall forfeit their renown
Adding immortal labours of his own—
Whether he traced historic truth, with zeal
For the State's guidance or the Church's weal,
Or fancy, disciplined by studious art,
Informed his pen, or wisdom of the heart,
Or judgments sanctioned in the Patriot's mind
By reverence for the rights of all mankind.
Wide were his aims, yet in no human breast
Could private feelings find a holier nest.
His joys, his griefs, have vanished like a cloud
From Skiddaw's top ; but he to heaven was vowed
Through a life long and pure ; and Christian faith
Calm'd in his soul the fear of change and death.

WOTOBANK.

Near the village of Beckermet, in West Cumberland, is a small mound, upon which stands a summer-house, known by the name of "Wotobank." The derivation of this name is assigned by tradition to the following incident :—

A Lord of Beckermet, with his Lady and servants, were one day hunting wolves. During the chase the lady was missing. After a long and painful search, her body was found on this mound or bank, mangled by a wolf, which was discovered in the act of tearing it to pieces. In the first transport of grief, the husband exclaimed, "Woe to this bank !"

" ' Woe to thee, Bank ! ' were the first words that burst,
'And be thy soil with bitter offspring curst !
Woe to thee, Bank, for thou art drunk with gore
The purest heart of woman ever bore !'
'Woe to thee, Bank !' the attendants echoed round,
And pitying shepherds caught the grief-fraught sound."

THE POPULAR HUNTING SONG, "JOHN PEEL."

[Written by John Woodcock Graves.]

D'ye ken John Peel, with his coat so gay?
D'ye ken John Peel, at the break of day?
D'ye ken John Peel, when he's far, far away,
With his hounds and his horn in the morning?

    CHORUS—
  'Twas the sound of his horn brought me from my bed,
  And the cry of his hounds, which he ofttimes led,
  For Peel's view-halloa would awaken the dead,
  Or the fox from his lair in the morning.

D'ye ken that hound whose voice is death?
D'ye ken her sons of peerless faith?
D'ye ken that a fox, with his latest breath,
Curs'd them all, as he died in the morning?
    CHORUS—'Twas the sound, &c.

Yes, I ken John Peel and auld Ruby too;
Ranter and Ringwood, and Bellman so true;*
From the drag to the chase, from the chase to the view,
From the view to the death in the morning.
    CHORUS—'Twas the sound, &c.

And I've follow'd John Peel both often and far,
O'er the rasper fence, and the gate and the bar,
From Low Denton side up to Scratchmere Scar,
When we vied for the brush in the morning.
    CHORUS—'Twas the sound, &c.

Then here's to John Peel from my heart and soul.
Come fill, fill to him a brimming bowl,
For we'll follow John Peel thro' fair or thro' foul,
While we're waked by his horn in the morning.
    CHORUS—'Twas the sound, &c.

Then here's to John Peel, from my heart and soul;
Let's drink to his health, let's finish the bowl,
We'll follow John Peel thro' fair and thro' foul,
If we want a good hunt in the morning.
    CHORUS—'Twas the the sound, &c.

D'ye ken John Peel, with his coat so gay
He liv'd at Caldbeck, once on a day;
Now, he has gone far, far away,
We shall ne'er hear his voice in the morning!
    CHORUS—'Twas the sound, &c.

---

* These were the real names of the hounds which Peel in his old age said were the very best he ever had or saw.

The music of the above song was arranged with symphonies by Mr. William Metcalfe, and sung by him at one of the annual dinners of the Cumberland Benevolent Institution in London.

"Old John Peel," writes "H. H. D.," in the *Gentleman's Magazine*, "was for many years the hunting hero of Cumberland, and the Cumbrians, who never met before, have grasped hands, and joyfully claimed county kindred in the Indian bungalow or the log-hut of the back woods, when one of them being called on for a song, struck up 'D'ye ken John Peel?' The popularity of the song has spread far and wide. It has been chanted in most parts of the world where English hunters have penetrated: it was heard in the soldiers' camp at Lucknow, and was lately sung before the Prince of Wales." Of the origin of the song, the author says:—"Nearly forty years have now passed away since John Peel and I sat in a snug parlour at Caldbeck, among the Cumbrian mountains. We were then both in the heyday of manhood, and hunters of the olden fashion: meeting the night before to arrange earth stopping, and in the morning to take the best part of the hunt—the drag over the mountains in the mist—while fashionable hunters still lay in the blankets. Large flakes of snow fell that evening. We sat by the fireside hunting over again many a good run, and recalling the feats of each particular hound, or narrow neck-break 'scapes, when a flaxen-haired daughter came in, saying, 'Father, what do they say to what Granny sings?' Granny was singing to sleep my eldest son with an old rant called *Bonnie Annie*.* The pen and ink for hunting appointments being on the table, the idea of writing a song to this old air forced itself upon me, and thus was produced impromptu, "*D'ye ken John Peel?*" Immediately after I sang it to poor Peel, who smiled through a

---

* "Bonnie Annie," or "Where will Bonnie Annie lie."

stream of tears which fell down his manly cheeks; and I well remember saying to him in a joking style, 'By jove, Peel, you'll be sung when we're both run to earth!'" "H. H. D." very happily remarks that "John seems to have come into this world only to send foxes out of it;" and after having hunted (as no other man could) a pack of fox hounds to the delight of all Cumberland for upwards of forty years, he died full of honours in 1854, at the ripe age of 78; and under the shadows of tall sycamores and yews in the quiet village churchyard of Caldbeck, may be seen his grave, surmounted by a memorial stone designed after true hunting fashion.

RYDAL.

Rydal Mount, a short distance above Rydal church, stands in a quiet secluded nook. It is a simple unpretending edifice, almost concealed by trees and shrubs. This was the poet's residence for thirty-seven years, and here he died on the 23rd of April, 1850, having attained his eightieth year. A beautiful view is obtained from the grassy mound in front, a portion of Windermere being visible over the lovely wooded Vale of Rothay.

KIRKSTONE PASS.

Near the summit of this pass is an inn (The Traveller's Rest), the highest inhabited house in England. It is 1475 feet above the sea. When descending into Patterdale, and on the left, is passed the stone which

"Gives to the savage pass its name."

It is not like a kirk or church from this side, but when seen from a point half-way down the pass it assumes that shape.

L—2

THE "OLD MAN," CONISTON.

On the summit of this mountain are three "men," or beacons of stone, a word equivalent to the Scottish "cairn," which are popularly known as the "Old Man," his "Wife," and his "Son;" and standing by the side of them on a clear day, the traveller can discover the bays and the estuaries of the Lancashire and a part of the Cumberland coast; the Isle of Man and Wales, and far off, indistinct, but perceptible, the peak of Snowdon, in Wales.

ESKDALE.

In this valley are the remains of what is supposed to have been a Roman fortress, now called by the inhabitants "Hardknott Castle."

> " * * * * that lone camp on Hardknott's height,
> Whose guardians bent the knee to Jove and Mars."

All that remains is an enclosure of about 300 feet square, surrounded by loose stones, with heaps of stones in the centre, and apparently at the corners are remains of towers.

THOMAS CARLYLE.

The late sage of Chelsea, in his "Sartor Resartus," says, "From this centre (Great Gable) of the mountain region, beautiful and solemn is the aspect to the traveller. He beholds a world of mountains, a hundred and a hundred savage peaks, like giant spirits of the wilderness; there in their silence, in their solitude, even as on the night when Noah's deluge first dried. He gazes over these stupendous masses with wonder, almost with longing desire; never till this hour has he known Nature, that she was one, that she was his mother and divine. A murmur of eternity and immensity, of death and of life, steals through his soul; and he feels as if death and life were one, as if the earth were not dead, as if the spirit of the earth had its throne in that splendour, and his own spirit were therewith holding communion."

AN OLD PIANO'S APOLOGY.

In the coffee room of the Prince of Wales' Lake Hotel, Grasmere, there is an old piano, the top of which is screwed down. One evening, a short time ago, a tourist forced the screws out and attempted to play, at the same time making some disparaging remarks on the quality of the instrument, adding that some of the lake poets, if any such were left, ought to write a poem in praise of that piano. Though but two other guests were present at the time, who had made a call in passing, the following lines were found on the key-board of the instrument on the following morning :—

> Stranger, forbear, rend not my case with force ;
> Were my days thine, thy case might still be worse.
> Like thee, I once was young—I should say new ;
> Like me, thou may'st be old—keep that in view ;
> Mock not my age, or raise the idle laugh
> At my expense, in language known as " chaff."
> In youth my nerves in unison were strung ;
> When lightly touched with silvery notes they rung.
> When not illused, no harsh or grating chord
> E'er issued from this ancient harpsichord ;
> E'er lake hotels, amid these hills were reared,
> In lordly mansions oft my tones were heard.
> Ladies of high degree, of wealth and beauty,
> Have shown me favour as a sacred duty ;
> Oft have my sounds with their sweet voices blended ;
> They're silent now—alas ! my charming's ended.
> Ask not of age, the strength or fire of youth,
> A well-worn life's a monument of truth ;
> And when you sneer at my attempts to sing,
> Remember a crack'd shilling yields no ring.
> Heap not on me thy undeserved abuse,
> Though I'm no more of ornament or use,
> But make allowance both for time and place ;
> Shun not a friend whose fault's a wrinkled face.
> Had you with care my circumstances viewed,
> You would have seen how badly I was screwed.

HELM CRAG, GRASMERE.

At the further end of Grasmere Lake, between the branches of Easdale and Greenburn, stands Helm Crag, distinguished, not so much by its height, as by its summit of broken rocks, which Mr. Gray likens to "some gigantic building demolished;" Mr. West, to "a mass of antediluvian ruins;" Mr. Green, to the figures of a "lion and a lamb;" Mr. Wordsworth, to an "astrologer and an old woman cowering;" Mr. Budworth, to a "number of stones jumbled together after the mystical manner of the Druids;" Mrs. Radcliffe says, "Helm Crag rears its crest—a strange fantastic summit, round, yet jagged and splintered;" and the traveller who views it from Dunmail Raise may think that a mortar elevated for throwing shells into the valley would be no unapt comparison. A road turns off on the left to the church, near which stands the ancient Red Lion Inn, respectably kept by Robert Newton and Sarah his wife, in 1792, when Captain Budworth and his friend, on "a fortnight's ramble to the lakes," had a bespoke dinner at tenpence a head.*

Helm Crag is one of the most noted mountains in the lake district. Many climb to the summit to have a closer inspection of those mysterious rocks which form such fantastic shapes.

The lion and lamb are very remarkable when seen from many points in the vale of Grasmere, and on looking from Dunmail Raise, the mortar is perfect.

---

* For the information of landlords, and the benefit of tourists, we are tempted to give the bill of fare on this occasion: "Roasted pike, stuffed—A boiled fowl—Veal cutlets and ham—Beans and bacon—cabbage—pease and potatoes—Anchovy sauce—parsley and butter—Plain butter—Butter and cheese—Wheat bread and oat cake—Three cups of preserved gooseberries, with a bowl of cream in the centre—for two people, at tenpence a head."

Wordsworth, writing of the " ancient woman, seated on Helm Crag," in the " Waggoner," says :—

> " The Astrologer, sage Sydrophel,
> Where at his desk and book he sits,
> Puzzling on high his curious wits ;
> He whose domain is held in common,
> With no one but the Ancient Woman,
> Cowering beside her rifted cell,
> As if intent on magic spell ;
> Dread pair, that, spite wind and weather,
> Still sit upon Helm Crag together."

THE WISHING GATE, GRASMERE.

It was the popular belief in the neighbourhood that any wish formed or expressed here would be fulfilled. The old gate, with the " moss-grown bar," has been replaced by one which is now covered with the initials of tourists.

> " * * * even the stranger from afar,
> Reclining on this moss-grown bar,
>   Unknowing and unknown,
> The infection of the ground partakes,
> Longing for his beloved, who makes
>   All happiness her own.

GRASMERE.

The Swan Hotel is noted for having been the point whence Scott, Wordsworth, and Southey commenced the ascent of Helvellyn. A small house at Lawn End, near the Prince of Wales's hotel, was for eight years the residence of Wordsworth, and afterwards occupied for a time by De Quincey. Not far distant is the *church*—the church of the " *Excursion.*" In a corner of the burying-ground, close to the river, are the graves of Wordsworth and his family, and of Hartley Coleridge.

LEVEN'S HALL.

The park here is well stocked with deer. The gardens were planned by Beaumont, gardener to James II., who, it is said, designed Hampton Court Gardens. They are laid out in the old Dutch style. The trees are cut and twisted about in most fantastical shapes. In the interior of the house are some interesting pictures, tapestry, and oak carvings. The carved decorations of one room are said to have cost at least £3,000.

STORR'S HALL, WINDERMERE.

Scott, Wordsworth, Southey, Canning, and Professor Wilson met here as the guests of the then proprietor, Mr. Bolton. The voyageur may picture in his mind the happy days when these celebrated men met, and Windermere glittered with all her sails in honour of the "Great Northern Minstrel."

TROUTBECK, WINDERMERE.

Professor Wilson writes of this picturesque village:— "The cottages stand for the most part in clusters of twos and threes, with here and there what in Scotland is called a clachan—many a sma' town within the ae lang town; but where, in all broad Scotland, is a wide, long, scattered congregation of rural dwellings, all dropped down where the painter and the poet would have wished to plant them, on knolls and in dells, on banks and braes, and below tree-crested rocks, and all bound together in picturesque confusion by old groves of ash, oak, and sycamore, and by flower gardens and fruit orchards, rich as those of the Hesperides."

LITTLE LANGDALE.

This place is in the midst of scenery described in Wordsworth's "Excursion," and the abode of the "*Solitary*" of that poem. The Langdale Pikes, those

> "Two huge peaks
> That from some other vale peer into this"

with magical effect, and stand nobly at the head of the valley. From no other point do they present so fine an appearance. After the "steep ascent,"

> "Behold,
> Beneath his feet, a little lowly vale,
> A lowly vale, and yet uplifted high
> Among the mountains; even as if the spot
> Had been, from eldest time by wish of theirs
> So placed,—to be shut out from all the world !
> Urn-like it was in shape, as deep as an urn;
> With rocks encompassed, save that to the south
> Was one small opening, where a heath-clad ridge
> Supplied a boundary less abrupt and close—
> A quiet, treeless nook, with two green fields,
> A liquid pool, that glittered in the sun,
> And one bare dwelling, one abode no more !
> It seemed the home of poverty and toil,
> Though not of want: the little fields made green
> By husbandry of many thrifty years,
> Paid cheerful tribute to the moorland house.
> There crows the cock, single in his domain;
> The small birds find in Spring no thicket there
> To shroud them; only from the neighbouring vales
> The cuckoo, straggling up to the hill-tops
> Shouteth faint tidings of some gladder place."

These words were written on the supposition that the spectator is looking down upon the valley, not from the road, but from one of its elevated sides. The stranger will also observe that the vale is no longer a "treeless nook," there being now fir and larch plantations. The

> "One bare dwelling; one abode no more,"

is seen at the foot of the vertical cliff called Side Pike.

SOUTHEY AND AUTOGRAPHY.

Southey, like Hartley Coleridge and other celebrated men, was frequently applied to by collectors of caligraphy and autographs; among the many was a Yankee, who kept an exhibition at Philadelphia, and modestly asked for Southey's painted portrait, "which is very worthy a place in my collection;" then a herdsman in the Vale of Clwyd requested permission to send specimens of prose and verse—his highest ambition was the acquaintance of learned men; then a lover requested him to make an acrostic on the name of a young lady—the lover's rival having beaten him in writing verses; enclosed was an honorarium. Southey's amiability at this point gave way; he did not write the acrostic, and the money he spent on blankets for poor women in Keswick. A society for the suppression of albums was proposed by Southey; yet sometimes he was captured in a gracious mood. Samuel Simpson, of Liverpool, begged for a few lines in his handwriting "to fill a vacancy in his collection of autographs, without which his series must remain for ever most incomplete." The laureate replied:—

> Inasmuch as you Sam, a descendant of Sim,
> For collecting hand-writings have taken a whim,
> And to me, Robert Southey, petition have made—
> In a civil and nicely-penned letter—post paid—
> That I to your album so gracious would be
> As to fill up a page there apportioned for me,
> Five couplets I send you, by aid of the Nine—
> They will cost you for postage a penny a line;
> At Keswick, October the sixth they were done,
> One thousand eight hundred and twenty and one."

HARTLEY COLERIDGE.

A Mr. Joseph Dearden, of Preston, who was an indefatigable collector of autographs, wrote to Mr. Hartley Coleridge, requesting him to procure him an autograph of the poet Wordsworth. The following was the waggish reply received, evidently written *impromptu* by Mr. Coleridge, who had been erroneously addressed in the applicant's letter as Mr. Collridge. It was about this time the poet Wordsworth's daughter died:—

"Nab, Dec. 18th, 1847.
"Dear Sir,—My surname 'Collridge' isn't,
I am a 'Coleridge' 'Hartley' christened.
The Bard that did revisit Yarrow
Is smitten with a household sorrow;
His only daughter, dear beloved,
Is from this vale of tears removed.
And therefore you, yourself, must see
'Twould be an inpropriety
For me, or any other chap,
To plague him for a single scrap.
Yet, Joseph, if your name had been
Not Joseph, but sweet Josephine,
Fanny—or Mary—or simple Meg,
I might have been so bold to beg
For a few traces of his pen;
But autograph-collecting men
I know are his abominations,
And so are all new corporations.
For, be't his weakness or his glory,
He is a stubborn auld-world Tory,
And would not choose his pen to stir
For corporation officer;
Though Joseph Dearden, 'tis by all allowed,
Is one of whom proud Preston may be proud."

ONLY ONE.

James Hogg, the Ettrick Shepherd, used to relate with much humorous relish an anecdote of the author of "*The Excursion.*" At a meeting in the house of Professor Wilson, on Windermere, in the autumn of 1817, where Wordsworth, Hogg, and several other poets were present, the evening became distinguished by a remarkably brilliant bow of the nature of the aurora borealis across the heavens. The party came out to see it, and looked on for some time in admiration. Hogg remarked, "It is a triumphal arch got up to celebrate this meeting of the poets." He afterwards heard the future poet laureate whispering unconsciously to himself, "Poets! poets! what does the fellow mean? Where are they?" In his conception, there was but one poet present.

SAMUEL TAYLOR COLERIDGE'S OPINION OF SCOTCH AND ENGLISH LAKES.

The five finest things in Scotland are:—(1) Edinburgh; (2) The Ante-chamber of the Fall of Foyers; (3) The view of Loch Lomond from Inch Tavannach, the highest of the islands; (4) The Trosachs; (5) The view of the Hebrides from a point, the name of which I forget. But the intervals between the five things in Scotland are very dreary, whereas in Cumberland and Westmorland there is a cabinet of beauties, each thing being beautiful in itself, and the very passage from one lake, mountain, or valley to another, is itself a beautiful thing again. The Scotch lakes are so like one another, from their great size, that in a picture you are obliged to read their names, but the English lakes, especially Derwent Water, or rather the whole vale of Keswick, is so rememberable, that, after having been once seen, no one ever requires to be told what it is when drawn. This vale is about as large a basin as Loch Lomond; the latter is covered with water, but in the former instance we have two lakes with a charming river to connect them, and lovely villages at the foot of the mountains, and other habitations, which give an air of life and cheerfulness to the whole place.

POPE'S LINES ON WINDSOR FOREST.

The following lines are very apropos to the English lake district, and well worthy of a place here:—

> Here hills and vales, the woodland and the plain,
> Here earth and water seem to strive again;
> Not chaos like, together crushed and bruised,
> But, as the world, harmoniously confused.

WYTHBURN.

The small inn and church at Wythburn, near the head of lake Thirlmere, is thus apostrophised by the late Mr. Hartley Coleridge, who lived and died at ivy-covered Nab Cottage, Rydal, and was interred in Grasmere churchyard :—

> Here, traveller, pause and think, and duly think
>   What happy, holy thoughts may heavenward rise,
> Whilst thou and thy good steed together drink,
>   Beneath this little portion of the skies.
>
> See! on one side a humble house of prayer,
>   Where silence dwells, a maid immaculate,
> Save when the Sabbath and the priest are there,
>   And some few souls for manna wait.
>
> Humble it is, meek, and very low,
>   And speaks its purpose by a single bell ;
> But God Himself, and He alone, can know
>   If spiry temples please Him half so well.

RUSH BEARING.

In Westmorland, Lancashire, and districts of Yorkshire, there is still celebrated between hay-making and harvest, a village fête called the rush-bearing. Young women, dressed in white, and carrying garlands of flowers and rushes, walk in procession to the parish church, accompanied by a crowd of rustics, with flags flying and music playing. There they suspend their floral chaplets on the chancel rails, and the day is concluded with a simple feast. Ambleside and Grasmere, in Westmorland, are still the chief strongholds of this popular practice. Hentzner, in his "*Itinerary*," says of Queen Elizabeth's presence chamber at Greenwich :—The floor, after the English fashion, was strewn with *hay*, meaning rushes. The strewing of rushes in the way where processions were to pass, is attributed by our poets to all times and countries. Thus, at the coronation of Henry V. when the procession was coming, the grooms cried:—

"More rushes, more rushes!"

Thus also at a wedding:

Full many maids, clad in their best array,
In honour of the bride, come with their flaskets
Fill'd full with flowers: others in wicker baskets
Bring from the marsh, rushes, to o'erspread
The ground, whereon to church the lovers tread.

They were used green:

Where is this stranger? Rushes, ladies, rushes!
Rushes as green as summer for this stranger!

The following is a poetical description of the "Rush-bearing" at Grasmere, photographs of which can be had from Mr. Baldry, Bookseller, &c., there:—

THE RUSH-BEARERS.

In Grasmere's hill-girt valley,
  When Summer's at the full,
The children of the dalesmen hold
  A pretty festival.

The Church of good St. Oswald
  Possessed in days of yore—
For the hardy race who worshipp'd there
  A rugged, earthen floor.

As we may well imagine
  This floor, so damp and cold,
Gave influenza to the young—
  Rheumatics to the old.

'Twas an outrage to all feeling
  (Especially of the shins)
To have to kneel in mud and mire
  When they confessed their sins!

And so, to make things pleasant,
  And save the doctor's fees,
They strewed the Church with rushes dry,
  And thus got warmth and ease.

But when they'd grown more polished,
   And grown their worldly store—
Discarding mother earth, and reeds,
   They made a wooden floor.
Yet still we know old customs
   Will round men's hearts entwine,
And once a year were rushes brought
   As in the "Auld Lang Syne."
But now they deck'd their burdens
   With flowers of every hue,
And hung them round the old Church walls
   And stuck them on each pew.
And the children of the valley
   To this day faithful keep
The custom of their hardy sires
   Who in the Churchyard sleep.
For when hot July's waning,
   They to the lake repair,
To pull the reeds and lilies white
   That grow in plenty there.
With these—and ferns and mosses,
   And flowers of varied dye,
They hasten home, and all day long
   Their busy fingers ply.
Then in the quiet evening,
   Ere dew begins to fall,
They range their floral trophies on
   The Churchyard's low-topp'd wall.
Here crosses without number,
   Of every shape and size,
And wreaths, triangles, crowns and shields,
   Appear in flow'ry guise!
And verses too, and mottoes,
   Words ta'en from Holy Writ—
And some designs which mock the pen,
   We'll call them nondescri(p)t.
But all are glad and happy
   Who in the pageant share,
And the urchins with the nondescripts
   Are proud as any there;
And proudly struts each youngster,
   When, devices gay in hand,
They round about the village march
   To the music of the band

Like to a string of rainbows
　　Appears that cortege bright,
Winding 'mong the crooked lanes,
　　In the golden evening light!

And coming to the Church again
　　They bear the garlands in,
And fix them round the time-stained fane,
　　While the bells make merry din.

But hark! before departing
　　From that house of prayer,
The incense of a grateful hymn
　　Floats on the quiet air!

And so the village pageant
　　Ends in sounds of peace—
We trust the time may never come
　　This pretty show shall cease!

RUSH-BEARERS' HYMN.

St. Oswalds', Grasmere.

Our Fathers to the House of God,
　　As yet a building rude,
Bore offerings from the flowery sod,
　　And fragrant rushes strewed.

May we, their children, ne'er forget
　　The pious lesson given,
But honour still, together met,
　　The Lord of Earth and Heaven.

Sing we the good Creator's praise,
　　Who gives us sun and showers,
To cheer our hearts with fruitful days,
　　And deck our world with flowers.

These, of the great Redeemer's grace,
　　Bright emblems here are seen;
He makes to smile the desert place
　　With flowers and rushes green.

All glory to the Father be,
　　All glory to the Son,
All glory, Holy Ghost, to Thee,
　　While endless ages run.—Amen:

Advertisements.

WILSON'S
ROYAL OAK HOTEL,
KESWICK.

This Hotel is the largest and oldest established FAMILY and COMMERCIAL HOTEL in town, being the principal Coaching House.

It has of late years been partially re-built and re-fitted, to meet modern requirements, and the Proprietor has Two Farms in connection, from which Fresh Butter, Cream, New-laid Eggs, &c., are supplied every morning.

There is also a large Posting Establishment belonging, upwards of Twenty Horses and Vehicles of every description regularly on hire. Coaches leave the Hotel every day for all parts of the Lake District.

HOT BATHS. ✢ BILLIARDS.

Wm. WILSON, Proprietor.

Advertisements.

WINDERMERE LAKE.

LAKE-SIDE
NEW HOTEL.

This Excellent Hotel is beautifully situated at the

FOOT OF THE LAKE,

ADJOINING

The Lake-side Station of the Furness Railway and Steamboat Pier.

CONVEYANCES & PLEASURE BOATS.

ADDRESS:

LAKE-SIDE NEW HOTEL,
VIÂ
CARNFORTH.

C. BROWN, Proprietor.

Advertisements.

SIMPSON'S
SCAWFELL HOTEL

ROSTHWAITE, BORROWDALE, KESWICK,

On the Direct Route from Keswick to Buttermere, nearest the Highest Mountains in England, of any Hotel in the Lake District; has good Accommodation and is newly fitted up.

GOOD TROUT FISHING FROM THE BANKS OF THE PLEASURE GROUND.

A splendid Lawn-Tennis and Croquet Ground and Baths have been added to the Establishment.

POST ARRIVES AT 11.30 A.M. AND LEAVES AT 3 P.M.

Conveyances, Mountain Ponies & Guides.

FAMILIES BOARDED BY WEEK OR MONTH.

GOOD STABLING AND COACH HOUSE.

A. SIMPSON, *Proprietress.*

THE LAKES, CUMBERLAND.

D. EASTON,
NAG'S HEAD HOTEL,
WYTHBURN,

Situate at the foot of Helvellyn, and at the head of Thirlmere Lake.

IT IS CENTRALLY PLACED FOR EXCURSIONS, AND FROM IT MAY BE MADE THE SHORTEST ASCENT TO HELVELLYN.

Post Horses, Mountain Ponies, & Guides

TO ALL PARTS OF THE LAKE DISTRICT.

GOOD FISHING IN THE NEIGHBOURHOOD.

Also, in connection with this Hotel, there are two Private Lodging Houses, close at the head of Thirlmere Lake. One contains three bed-rooms, sitting-rooms, kitchens, stable, &c.; the other has six bed-rooms, drawing-room dining-room, and kitchen.

Advertisements.

STOREY'S PRIVATE HOTEL,

ST. JOHN'S STREET, KESWICK.

LAKE AND MOUNTAIN SCENERY.

THE ECHOES
OF THE
LAKES AND MOUNTAINS

May be had, Price 1/6 & 2/-, in the Lake District, from the following:

Mr. GARNETT, Stationer, Windermere.
Mr. NICHOLLS, Bazaar, Bowness.
Messrs. BRUNSKILL, Photographers, Bowness.
ROYAL HOTEL, Bowness.
Messrs. ATKINSON & SONS, Bankers & Drapers, Bowness.
Mr. BARKER, Steamboat Pier, Bowness.
LAKE-SIDE RAILWAY STATION (foot of), Windermere.
Mr. WEARING, Steamboat Pier, Ambleside.
Mr. HOULDIN, Bookseller and Newsvendor, Ambleside.
The Misses GRIER, Stationers, &c., Ambleside.
Mr. EWINGTON, Bookseller, &c., Post Office, Ambleside.
Mr. HODGSON, Stationer, Post Office, Grasmere.
Mr. BALDRY, Stationer and Photographer, Grasmere.
NAG'S HEAD, Wythburn, Thirlmere.
PETTIT'S Art Gallery, St. John's Street, Keswick.
Mr. ABRAHAMS, Photographer, &c., Lake Road, Keswick.
Messrs. HOGARTH & HAYES, Southey Hill Pencil Works, Keswick.
STOREY'S HOTEL, St. John's Street, Keswick.
CLARK'S Cedar Goods & Stationery Warehouse, Keswick.
KING'S BAZAAR, Main Street, Keswick.
FISH HOTEL, Buttermere.
VICTORIA HOTEL, Buttermere.
Mr. SCOTT, Bookseller, "Observer" Office, Penrith.
Mr. MOSCROP, Bookseller, Stationer, &c., Burrowgate, Penrith.

And of any Bookseller.

www.ingramcontent.com/pod-product-compliance
Lightning Source LLC
Chambersburg PA
CBHW020308170426
43202CB00008B/532